THE COMPLETE NORDIC COOKBOOK

2 Books in 1: Over 100 Recipes For
Authentic Scandinavian Food

Adele Tyler

Maki Blanc

NORDIC
COOKBOOK

Discover 77 Recipes for Cooking at Home Traditional and Modern Scandinavian Dishes

---

Adele Tyler

© Copyright 2020 by (Adele Tyler) - All rights reserved.

This document is geared towards providing exact and reliable information in regards to the topic and issue covered. The publication is sold with the idea that the publisher is not required to render accounting, officially permitted, or otherwise, qualified services. If advice is necessary, legal or professional, a practiced individual in the profession should be ordered.

- From a Declaration of Principles which was accepted and approved equally by a Committee of the American Bar Association and a Committee of Publishers and Associations.

It is not legal in any way to reproduce, duplicate, or transmit any part of this document in either electronic means or in printed format. Recording of this publication is strictly prohibited and any storage of this document is not allowed unless with written permission from the publisher. All rights reserved.

The information provided herein is stated to be truthful and consistent, in that any liability, in terms of inattention or otherwise, by any usage or abuse of any policies, processes, or directions contained within is the solitary and utter responsibility of the recipient reader. Under no circumstances will any legal responsibility or blame be held against the publisher for any reparation, damages, or monetary loss due to the information herein, either directly or indirectly.

Respective authors own all copyrights not held by the publisher.

The information herein is offered for informational purposes solely and is universal as so. The presentation of the information is without a contract or any type of guarantee assurance.

The trademarks that are used are without any consent, and the publication of the trademark is without permission or backing by the trademark owner. All trademarks and brands within this book are for clarifying purposes only and are owned by the owners themselves, not affiliated with this document.

CONTENTS

INTRODUCTION _____ 11

CHAPTER 1: INTRODUCTION TO NORDIC CUISINE __ 13

1.1 1.1 History of Nordic Foods _____ 13

1.2. Vikings Background _____ 14

1.3 Interesting Facts _____ 15

1.4 Nutrition Facts _____ 16

1.5 Nordic Food Trends _____ 17

1.6 Essential Ingredients to Prepare at Home _____ 18

CHAPTER 2: CLASSIC SWEDISH RECIPES _____ 19

2.1 Swedish Meatballs _____ 21

2.2 Old-Fashioned Gingersnaps _____ 22

2.3 Quick Cream of Mushroom Soup _____ 24

2.4 Swedish Rye Bread _____ 25

2.5 Cheese and Herb Potato Fans _____ 26

2.7 No-Bake Chocolate Cookies _____ 30

2.8 Swedish Sticky Chocolate Cake _____ 30

2.9 Almond Tarts _____ 32

2.10 Chocolate Swiss Roll Cake _____ 34

2.11 Summer Berry Tart _____ 36

2.12 Almond cake _____ 38

CHAPTER 3: POPULAR DANISH DISHES _____ 47

3.2 Cured Salmon _____ 49

3.3 Fish Filet with Dill Crème Fraiche _____ 51

3.4 Danish Liver Paté _____ 52

3.5 Tongue Salad _____ 54

3.6 Brunette Kartofler _____ 55

3.7 Fried Pork And Parsley Sauce _____ 55

3.8 Danish Rice Dessert _____ 57

3.9 Danish Meatballs _____ 60

3.10 Danish Roast Pork With Cracking _____ 61

3.11 Danish Cold Buttermilk Soup _____ 63

3.12 Danish Breaded Pork Patties _____ 64

3.13 Danish Red Berry Pudding _____ 65

3.14 Danish Apple Cake _____ 66

3.15 Danish Chicken Tartlet _____ 67

3.16 Danish Rye Bread _____ 68

3.17 Danish Meatloaf _____ 70

CHAPTER 4: ICELAND FOOD RECIPES _____ 72

4.1 Prawn Paella _____ 72

4.2 Beef And Roasted Veg Lasagna _____ 73

4.3 Beef Enchiladas _____ 74

4.4 Fish Finger Pie _____ 76

4.5 Kuromame Sweetened Black Soybean _____ 77

4.6 Superboost Smoothie _____ 78

4.7 Beef Chili Nachos _____ 79

3.8 Berry Crumble _____ 81

4.9 Super Veg Cottage Pie _____ 82

4.10 Superboost Soup _____ 83

4.11 Beefy Baked Bean Pie _____ 84

4.12 Tasty Chicken Curry _____ 86

4.13 Secret Ingredient Chocolate Cake _____ 87

4.14 Cheat's Berry Brulee _____ 89

4.15 Sunday Roast _____ 89

4.16 Fruity Cakes _____ 91

4.16 Bangers And Cheesy Mustard Mash _____ 92

4.17 Chicken Pesto Tart _____ 93

4.18 Friday Night Kebabs _____ 94

CHAPTER 5: TRADITIONAL VIKINGS RECIPES _____ 95

5.4 Meatballs with Celeriac and Apples _____ 100

5.5 Kringle Recipe _____ 102

5.6 Shaved Winter Vegetables Salad _____ 104

5.7 Chocolate Cake _____ 106

5.8 Finnish Salmon Soup _____108

5.9 Icelandic Pancakes _____109

5.10 Midsummer Cocktail _____110

5.3 Rosemary and Thyme Roasted Rsdishes _____114

5.4 Jansson's Temptation _____115

CHAPTER 1: THE WORLD OF INSTANT POT SWEDISH DISHES RECIPES _____122

1.1 Ikea Swedish Meatballs Recipe _____122

1.2 Pepparkakor (Swedish Ginger Cookies) Recipe _____124

1.3 Swedish Apple Pie Recipe _____125

1.4 Swedish Potato Pancakes Recipe _____126

1.5 Swedish Rye Bread Recipe _____128

1.6 Swedish Blueberry Soup Recipe _____129

1.7 Swedish Ligonberry Sauce Recipe _____130

1.8 Crispy Hasselback Potatoes with Rosemary and Garlic Recipe _____131

1.9 Swedish Pancakes Recipe _____132

1.10 Swedish Rice Porridge Recipe _____134

1.11 Swedish Semlor Buns Recipe _____135

1.12 Swedish Almond Tarts Recipe _____136

1.13 Swedish Visiting Cake Recipe _____137

1.14 Swedish Cinnamon Rolls Recipe _____139

1.15 Swedish Thumbprint Cookies Recipe _____140

1.16 Swedish Fika Recipe _____ 141

1.17 Traditional Swedish Glogg Recipe _____ 143

1.18 Vegan Swedish Yellow Split Pea Soup Recipe _____ 144

1.19 Braised Swedish Red Cabbage Recipe _____ 145

1.20 Swedish Cheese Pie Recipe _____ 146

1.21 Traditional Swedish Saffron Buns Recipe _____ 148

1.22 Swedish Potato and Anchovy Casserole Recipe _____ 149

1.23 Swedish Spinach Soup Recipe _____ 151

1.24 Swedish Crisp Bread Recipe _____ 152

1.25 Swedish Fish Soup with Saffron Rouille Recipe ___ 153

CHAPTER 2: THE WORLD OF INSTANT POT DANISH RECIPES _____ 156

2.1 Danish Caramelized Browned Potatoes Recipe _____ 156

2.2 Danish Meatballs Recipes _____ 157

2.3 Danish Chicken and Asparagus Tartlets Recipe _____ 159

2.4 Danish Open Faced Sandwiches Recipe _____ 161

2.5 Agurkesalat (Danish Cucumber Salad) Recipe _____ 162

2.6 Danish Rye Bread Recipe _____ 163

2.7 Danish Roasted Pork Recipe _____ 164

2.8 Danish Kringle Recipe _____ 166

2.9 Danish Potato Salad Recipe _____ 167

2.10 Danish Buttermilk Dessert Recipe _____ 168

2.11 Danish Breaded Pork Patties Recipe _____ **170**

2.12 Danish Red-berry Pudding with Cream Recipe _____ **171**

2.13 Classic Danish Hotdogs Recipe _____ **172**

2.14 Danish Meatloafs Recipe _____ **174**

2.15 Danish Apple Pork Recipe _____ **175**

2.16 Danish Red Cabbage Recipe _____ **177**

2.17 Danish Remoulade Recipe _____ **179**

2.18 Danish Sillsallet (Herring Salad) Recipe _____ **180**

2.19 Danish Breakfast Hash Recipe _____ **181**

2.20 Danish Pancakes Recipe _____ **182**

2.21 Danish Scalloped Potatoes Recipes _____ **184**

2.22 Danish Creamy Pastry Recipe _____ **185**

2.23 Danish Cream Puffs Recipe _____ **187**

2.24 Danish Dream Cake Recipe _____ **188**

2.25 Danish Risalamande Recipe _____ **189**

CHAPTER 3: THE WORLD OF INSTANT POT
NORWEGIAN RECIPES _____ **191**

3.1 Norwegian Fish Soup Recipe _____ **191**

3.2 Norwegian Waffles Recipe _____ **192**

3.3 Norwegian Meatballs Recipe _____ **194**

3.4 Norwegian Lefse Recipe _____ **195**

3.5 Norwegian Surkal Recipe _____ **197**

3.6 Norwegian Sveler Recipe _____ 198

3.7 Norwegian Potato Dumplings Recipe _____ 199

3.8 Norwegian Salmon with Dill Sauce Recipe _____ 201

3.9 Norwegian Porridge Recipe _____ 202

3.10 Norwegian Almond Cake Recipe _____ 204

CHAPTER 4: THE WORLD OF INSTANT POT FINNISH RECIPES _____ 205

4.1 Finnish Cabbage Casserole Recipe _____ 206

4.2 Finnish Salmon Soup Recipe _____ 207

4.3 Finnish Blueberry Pie Recipe _____ 210

4.4 Finnish Meatballs Recipe _____ 211

4.5 Finnish Pannu Kakku Recipe _____ 212

4.6 Finnish Pancakes Recipe _____ 214

4.7 Finnish Dried Pea Soup Recipe _____ 215

4.8 Finnish Doughnuts Recipe _____ 217

4.9 Finnish Cardamom Rolls Recipe _____ 218

4.10 Finnish Cinnamon Pastries Recipe _____ 220

CONCLUSION _____ 221

Introduction

Denmark, Sweden, Finland, Norway, and Iceland are part of the Nordic Region, the Greenland, Faroe Islands, and Åland. Denmark is a tiny, heavily populated country, the southernmost of the Nordic countries, making up many islands lined with beautiful beaches. Lakes and trees characterize the extensive Finnish landscape. Finland is also known for smartphones, art, and Moomins. The Volcanic Island of the North Atlantic, Iceland, is known for its hot springs and spectacular scenery. Norway is associated with oil and hills, for many. Its stunning, majestic terrain extends from the beach and peaks in the south to the North Cape's midnight sun across the east's rugged areas.

In the Nordic Countries, the largest nation is also the one with the highest population. Sweden is, for many, associated with the manufacture of high-quality vehicles, iron, and steel. The food of northern Scandinavia and the Sami citizens focuses on the few Arctic and sub-Arctic products, primarily reindeer, salmon, and berries.

The largest Nordic people had such restricted variety of ingredients before contemporary days, especially from the far north. Famines have been going on as early as the 19th century. While the industrial revolution arrived late, dining in the Nordic countries in the modern era has become very multicultural. Many traditional foods are focused on what used to be the diet of poor citizens, such as herring, dried cod, potatoes, and hard bread. Many have gained a certain sophistication and are now viewed as classy enough to be freely eaten by the middle or even upper-class citizens.

In the Nordic countries, picking fruit, picking mushrooms, hunting, and fishing are very popular activities, and the first three are readily accessible to foreigners. Almost anywhere there is suitable land for berry picking, and the right of access permits mushroom and such foraging. Fishing is also freely available, although other lure fishing licenses are often easy to obtain. Noma, perhaps the most popular restaurant in the world, opened in 2003 with the ambition of providing a modern take on the Nordic cuisine. Nordic cuisine has many nutritional benefits, as well.

"Nordic Cookbook" has five chapters with an introduction and some delicious Nordic recipes. Chapter one will convey the history of Nordic countries and Vikings, interesting facts about Nordic cuisine, nutritional information, and preparing Nordic food at home. Chapter two is about Swedish traditional and Fika recipes. Chapter three and four will cover Danish and Iceland recipes. In the last chapter, ancient Viking recipes are described to make you enjoy the ancient Nordic foods. Explore more about Nordic cuisine by reading this book now.

Chapter 1: Introduction to Nordic Cuisine

Because of its nutritional advantages, the Nordic diet is contrasted with the Mediterranean diet. According to outlets like Authority Nutrition, it contains less glucose, less salt, half the fiber, and double the fish and seafood relative to a normal Western diet. Some berries have been shown to possess high amounts of omega-3 fatty acids, and cholesterol may be reduced through diets rich in fish oil. Cold-pressed rapeseed is also proven to be as safe as virgin olive oil. To understand more about Nordic food, let's look at history and facts.

1.1 1.1 History of Nordic Foods

Nordic cuisine's heritage depends largely on its Viking background. But the conventional household cooking that provides the basis for the Modern Nordic Cuisine is also present. As oceans cover the Nordic countries, ocean fishing is a large part of these nations' food culture. Whaling in this area is also very high too. Not are whales used for commercial consumption, but they are also consumed in the Nordic countries. An instance of a whale steak came to notice. Scandinavians believe that it could be as delicious as beef if cooked properly.

Other than fish, the most prevalent meal in these countries is frequent catches carried by fishermen. Mostly, salmon and cod are preferred. Pork is the predominant choice when we search for meat on land. Cured, dried, baked, grilled, or roasted, pork is preserved in several ways. Potatoes, fresh spices, beetroot, mushrooms, wild berries, strawberries, imported European fruits like plums, and other imported products are stored, and fruits and vegetables go.

Nordic Cuisine relies more on the ingredients than on sauces. The biggest key is the freshness of the products. The lack of "heavy-butter sauce" in the French style keeps the products' emphasis, as though the ingredients are not great; there is nothing to cover up the poor taste in the dish. When it applies to deserts, a significant proportion of Nordic sweets are pastries. The desserts are strong and very sweet, in addition to the main dishes and many others. To keep the purchaser warm in the winter, they are presumably extremely sweet.

1.2. Vikings Background

The Viking Age was not a time to think about food's fat quality. The Vikings needed all the nutrition that they could get, particularly in winter, in the form of fat. A large part of their diet was beef, fish, fruits, cereals, and dairy products. In the shape of seeds, fruits, and honey, sweet food was eaten. The Vikings were also portrayed as gluttonous in England. According to the Englishmen, they drank and ate so much. The housework needed to be prepared and tailored to the various seasons during the Viking period. A farmer with agricultural animals and crops in the field, the average Viking was self-sufficient. Some people did not develop any of their food and also wanted to purchase it. The blacksmith or fisherman might fulfill his nutritional needs by purchasing or selling goods on the local market.

Every class of civilization, from kings to popular mariners, consumed meat every day was a big advantage of the Viking diet. This may mostly have been pork, as animals were easy to raise and fast to mature, but the Vikings often consumed beef, meat, and livestock.

Horses were also bred for food, a tradition that later led to disputes with Christian officials since, under church belief, horsemeat was a prohibited food.

The Vikings were avid hunters, trapping reindeers, elks, and even bears to get the flames back to the hearth. Although, of course, because the Vikings spent a lot of time on the sea, most of their diet was made up of seafood. Herrings were numerous and prepared in various ways: roasted, salted, grilled, pickled, and even whey preserved.

There were several big drawbacks, considering the overall healthy essence of the Viking diet. From archaeological digs of Viking cesspits and sewer systems, most Vikings struggled from parasites in their digestive tract: they had worms, simply put. The same pulpit excavations showed indigestible seeds consumed by Vikings from all the wheat-baked goods, some of which came from plants that are particularly harmful to humans.

1.3 Interesting Facts

This region of the world is full of seas, rivers, fjords, forestry, and agricultural fields, which have formed the base of the Scandinavian diet over the centuries. You will find that, for example, certain items, such as berries and seafood, are commonly available in the region, mirrored in each nation's dishes. You will also note that a few countries in their diets are very similar-Finland was once a member of Sweden, for instance, so their common dishes are bound to have similarities. Let's look more closely at interesting facts about the Nordic region:

Norway: They are masters of seafood (particularly fish, salmon, and crabs) as described, but you will also see lots of reindeer, lamb, cheese, berries, mushrooms, potatoes cabbage.

Sweden: Lingonberries are certainly a Swedish favorite, and they enjoy their salmon, potatoes, beef, and pork (which you will need for their famed meatballs!) as well.

Iceland: It is no wonder that fish is a big part of the local cuisine covered by ocean, but you will also see plenty of lambs, skyr (yogurt-like), rye flatbread, and berries.

Finland: They enjoy lingonberries, such as the Swedes, yet bilberries, beef, pork, reindeer, mushrooms, salmon, rye bread, and potato are equally common.

Denmark: For the Danes, who enjoy their pork, sausage, rye bread, leafy vegetables, cabbage, salmon, and potatoes, it is typically a hearty diet. Yes, and without a shout at the popular smørrebrød, you cannot even mention Danish cuisine!

Of course, the sweeter stuff in life is enjoyed by all of Scandinavia and the Nordic countries! You will note that they use many kinds of butter, honey, milk, cinnamon, cardamom, and saffron in their sweets, biscuits, and cookies.

.

1.4 Nutrition Facts

The Mediterranean diet is recognized for its correlation with a lower prevalence of chronic diseases such as type 2 diabetes and heart disease. Although there is not enough study on the Nordic diet to make those arguments, the concept is very similar: eat plenty of vegetables, whole grains, legumes, fish, and eat red meat and desserts comfortably. It is not shocking when we start breaking down the Nordic diet to be good for our health. It highlights whole grains that provide nutrition, vitamins, minerals, and nutrients. It is filled with vegetables and fruits that also provide essential nutrients such as vitamins A, C, E, calcium, and fiber. Several small studies have shown that the Nordic diet can help relieve blood pressure. In people with average cognition, the Nordic diet can also help preserve cognition.

1.5 Nordic Food Trends

Here are some of the trends in Nordic cuisine that you need to explore.

Unique and Unconventional Ingredients

Nordic-inspired flavours will modify the whole eating experience. For example, Barnängen can provide you with a sense of Swedish food.

It comprises multiple seeds, spices, and nutritious foods that have been on for a long time in the Swedes.

Fermenting Meat and Sausages

The beef and sausages that are fermented or curated also go perfectly with burgers and hot dogs. You are supposed to have an exciting meaty adventure filled with Nordic salad.

Smoked Food

Nordic countries see foraging as a chance to communicate with the world and to find free food for cooking. The thought of foraging is what most people would enjoy.

Foraging for Food

One of the Nordic cuisine phenomena that you will fall in love with is Smorrebrod. The open sandwich is often synonymous with toast with avocado, although it is unique in the Nordic countries.

Preservation of Produce

There is a special way for the Nordic countries to store their food for the winter months. It is a trend going on for decades, and you can only hope they have mastered the craft by now.

1.6 Essential Ingredients to Prepare at Home

Modern Scandinavian cuisine has been increasingly popular all over the world in recent times. Cloudy hills, open spaces, dense woods with fresh and refreshing air, and clean water define our Nordic scenery. The main ingredients in our Nordic Kitchens are deer, elk, sheep, berries, fruit, and mushroom, as well as seafood of several kinds. One of the key features of modern Scandinavian cooking is elegance. Nordic cuisine is based on fewer ingredients and higher-quality ingredients grown in the hot and dry Nordic climate, which affects the ingredients' taste. While preparing Nordic food at home, you have to collect some basic ingredients that are:

- Apples
- Ramson
- Cloudberries
- Blueberries
- Nordic trout
- Crayfish
- Icelandic skyr
- Mirabelle plum
- Herring
- Erica honey
- Elderflower
- Lamb meat

- Buckthorn berries
- Penny bun mushrooms
- Truffles
- Rye

If a new diet promises to offer supreme health advantages, you do not have to fully revise the eating pattern; if it is rich in fruits, veggies, lean protein, whole grains, and legumes, the Nordic Diet is, then it is sure to be healthy. Without totally exhausting yourself in the phase, your job is to work out how to fit some of your lifestyle values. Know, every day, and your dietary preferences can only eat up a limited portion of your total mental capacity. Step back, take some deep breaths, and try not to overanalyze it if you waste too long debating whether or not to get grain or rye bread.

Chapter 2: Classic Swedish Recipes

Rather than the sweet oats or additionally filling bacon and egg dishes that fill in as the cornerstone of numerous American breakfast menus, Japanese morning meals centre on pungent, appetizing flavours that fulfil and empower you for the afternoon.

The components of this hearty-yet-not-too-filling breakfast might seem more like lunch or dinner to Americans, and that is by design.

2.1 Swedish Meatballs

Cooking Time: 20 minutes
Serving Size: 3 dozen

Ingredients:
- 1 tablespoon lemon juice
- Canned lingonberries
- 1-¾ cups evaporated milk (divided)
- ½ cup of cold water
- 2 teaspoons beef granules
- 1 cup boiling water
- 2 tablespoons flour
- ½ teaspoon allspice
- ¾ cup chopped onion
- 1 pound lean ground beef
- 2 teaspoons butter
- ¼ cup fine dry bread crumbs
- ½ teaspoon salt
- Dash pepper

Method:
1. Apply the dry ingredients to two to three cups of evaporated milk.
2. Remove beef; lightly blend. Until cooled, refrigerate.
3. Form the meat mixture to 1-in with greasy fingers.

4. Heat the butter in a frying pan over medium heat. In quantities, brown meatballs.
5. Use hot water to remove the bouillon. Pour the meatballs over; put them to a boil. Cover; cook for fifteen minutes.
6. In the meantime, stir the cool water and the flour separately.
7. Remove meatballs from the skillet; trim the fat, conserve the liquids.
8. Cook, uncovered, over low heat, swirling until sauce thickens; add flour mixture and remaining evaporated milk to pan juices.
9. Placed the meatballs back in the skillet. Stir in the juice from the lemon.
10. Cover with lingonberries, if needed.

2.2 Old-Fashioned Gingersnaps

Cooking Time: 25 minutes

Serving Size: 4

Ingredients:

- ¼ teaspoon salt
- Additional sugar
- ¾ cup butter (softened)
- 1 teaspoon cloves
- 1 teaspoon ginger
- 2 cups flour
- 1 cup of sugar

- 2 teaspoons baking soda
- 1 teaspoon cinnamon
- 1 large egg
- ¼ cup molasses

Method:
1. Cream the butter and sugar by stirring and mixing in a mug.
2. Whisk in the molasses and egg.
3. Incorporate the flour, baking soda, cinnamon, garlic, salt, and ginger; apply it to the creamed solution. Cool in refrigerator.
4. Flip to 1-1/4-inch. Then dip the balls in sugar.
5. Place 2 inside, apart from ungreased sheets for baking.
6. Bake for about ten minutes at 375 ° or until fixed and the surface cracks. On wire shelves, cool.

2.3 Quick Cream of Mushroom Soup

Cooking Time: 30 minutes

Serving Size: 6

Ingredients:

- 2 cans of chicken broth
- 1 cup half-and-half cream
- 2 tablespoons butter
- ½ teaspoon salt
- ⅛ teaspoon pepper
- ½ pound mushrooms
- 6 tablespoons all-purpose flour
- ¼ cup (chopped) onion

Method:

1. Heat butter over moderate heat in a large frying pan; sauté the mushrooms and onions until soft.
2. Mix the flour, spice, peppers, and 1 can broth until smooth; mix well with the mushroom mixture.
3. Stir the remaining can of broth into it.
4. Carry to a boil; cook and stir for about 2 minutes, until caramelized. Reduce heat; add milk.
5. Simmer, uncovered, until the flavors are combined, about 15 minutes, periodically stirring.

2.4 Swedish Rye Bread

Cooking Time: 30 minutes

Serving Size: 4

Ingredients:
- 3-¾ cups all-purpose flour
- 2 tablespoons butter (melted)
- 1 package active dry yeast
- 2 teaspoons salt
- 2-½ cups rye flour
- 1-¾ cups warm water (divided)
- ¼ cup packed brown sugar
- 2 tablespoons shortening
- ¼ cup molasses

Method:
1. Dissolve the yeast in a dish of ¼ of a cup of sugar.
2. Stir well, add butter, molasses, reducing salts and remaining water.
3. Incorporate rye flour; beat until flat. To shape a soft dough, add ample all-purpose flour.
4. Turn to a baking sheet; knead for 6-8 minutes until soft and elastic.
5. Put in a lubricated cup to oil the end, rotating once.
6. Cover and let it rise until doubled, around 1-½ hours, in a hot spot.
7. Shape it into four circular loaves. Place on baking sheets that are greased.

8. Cover and let develop, 45-60 minutes, once doubled.
9. Bake for 30-35 minutes at 350° until lightly browned. Use butter to brush.

2.5 Cheese and Herb Potato Fans

Cooking Time: 75 minutes

Serving Size: 8

Ingredients:

- ½ cup Parmesan cheese (shredded)
- 2 tablespoons chives
- 8 medium potatoes
- ½ teaspoon pepper
- ¾ cup cheddar cheese (shredded)
- ½ cup butter (melted)
- Thyme
- 2 teaspoons salt
- Sage

Method:

1. Preheat the oven to 425 degrees.
2. Trim each potato crosswise into ⅛-inch with a paring blade.
3. Slices, keeping slices connected at the bottom; slightly fan the potatoes and put in a 13x9-in oil dish for baking.

4. Combine the sugar, salt, and black pepper in a shallow saucepan and drizzle over the potatoes.
5. Cook, uncovered, for 50-55 minutes or until soft.
6. Toss the cheese with the herbs in a small bowl; scatter over the potatoes.
7. Bake for 5 more minutes or until the cheese melts.

2.6 Spicy Sticky Cinnamon Rolls with Cream Cheese Icing

Cooking Time: 2 hours and 40 minutes

Serving Size: 24 rolls

Ingredients:

For the Dough

- 1 teaspoon salt
- 4 ½ to 5 cups flour
- 2 ¼ teaspoons dry yeast
- 2 large eggs
- 1 tablespoon vanilla extract
- 1 ¼ cups milk
- 6 tablespoons butter
- ½ cup of sugar

For the Icing

- ½ teaspoon vanilla
- ½ cup milk or cream
- 1 cup powdered sugar
- 4 ounces cream cheese

For the Filling
- 1 cup dark brown sugar
- 1 cup unsalted butter
- 4 cinnamon sticks
- ½ teaspoon cardamom seeds
- 1-star anise pod
- 1 teaspoon coriander seeds

Method:
1. Spray 1½ teaspoon of yeast in the mixing bowl over ¼ cup of lukewarm milk to create the dough and set it aside for five minutes until mildly bubbly.
2. Beat in half a cup of sugar, six tablespoons of melted butter, two big eggs, one teaspoon of vanilla, and one dash of salt using a stick blender's paddle attachment.
3. Stir in the flour, cup at a time, four halves to 5 cups, until the dough is moist and a little sticky.
4. Turn to the dough hooks and knead for five minutes or until the flour clears the blender's side and is firm and smooth in the stick blender.
5. Alternatively, knead for five to six minutes or until soft and stretchy on a floured worktop by hand.
6. Gently coat the dough and bowl with melted butter. Shape the dough into a ball and put it in

a greased bowl, turning it over to ensure that it is oil-coated.

7. Cover with cling film and grow until doubled, around 2 hours, in a warm location.
8. Grind the spices in a spice mixer until perfect for the filling and blend with brown sugar.
9. If you want to miss the extra cloves or use ground cinnamon rather than the whole, swap all the spice with 3 or 4 teaspoons of cinnamon.
10. Soften butter in a blender or with hand beaters along with the spice and sugars.
11. Grease two 9-inch layer pans gently. Roll the dough into a large rectangle on a lightly oiled board, about 14 centimeters by 24 inches.
12. Sprinkle it thickly with the cream sauce butter, and sugar as the dough is spread out, making sure to stretch it almost to the corners.
13. Roll up, stretching and drawing the dough into a taut and strong roll around the long side. To cut it into 24 separate rolls, use a table scraper or knife.
14. Divide the rolls between the prepared plates and let them rise for 45 to 60 minutes in a warm position before the rolls double in size.
15. As the rolls rise, heat the oven to 350F. For 20 to 30 minutes, bake the rolls.
16. Keeping their heat is the easiest way to assess doneness; they are finished around 190 and 200F.
17. Beat the sour cream, milk, syrup, and sugar together for the coating, adding more icing sugar if required to achieve the consistency you want.
18. Drizzle with a fork over the hot rolls. Serve it sweet.

2.7 No-Bake Chocolate Cookies

Cooking Time: 20 minutes

Serving Size: 7

Ingredients:

- 1 tablespoon coffee
- coconut
- 2 tablespoons cocoa powder
- ½ tablespoon vanilla extract
- 1 ½ cups oatmeal
- 6 tablespoons butter
- ¼ cup of sugar

Method:

1. Combine butter, honey, grains, vanilla, cocoa powder, and coffee (remember you never use instant boxes).
2. Roll the length of a meatball into balls.
3. To decorate, roll balls in almond or crystal sugar.
4. Eat right now, or if you want a tougher consistency, refrigerate or freeze.

2.8 Swedish Sticky Chocolate Cake

Cooking Time: 1 hour 45 minutes

Serving Size: 8

Ingredients:

- 1 tablespoon vanilla extract
- ½ cup butter (melted)
- 2 eggs
- 1 ⅓ cups white sugar
- ¼ cup of cocoa powder
- 1 pinch salt
- ½ cup all-purpose flour

Method:

1. Preheat the oven to 300 F degrees Celsius.
2. Grease an 8-inch pie plate gently.
3. Sift the rice, cocoa powder, and salts together; set it aside.
4. Stir the sugars into the eggs until they are smooth.
5. Apply the mixture of flour and whisk only once mixed.
6. Pour in the oil and vanilla extract; stir until well mixed.
7. Pour into a ready-made pie dish.
8. Bake for thirty minutes on the lower rack of the oven or until the middle is partially fixed.
9. Enable the cake to cool on the pie plate for one hour.
10. Serve warm or, nightly, refrigerate, and serve cold.

2.9 Almond Tarts

Cooking Time: 120 minutes

Serving Size: 1 tart

Ingredients:

Dough

- 2 teaspoons whole cardamom
- One small egg
- 7 oz. butter
- ¼ cup of organic cane sugar
- 2 cups flour

Filling

- ½ cup of organic cane sugar
- 3 small eggs
- One cup blanched almond.
- 2.5 oz. butter
- 2 bitter almonds

Icing

- ¼ cup confectioner's sugar
- Juice from an orange

Method:

1. Soften butter, sugar, and eggs together in a big, wide dish. This can be done either in the pan or directly on a clear countertop using your fingertips, mixing in flour.

2. Grind the cardamom as finely as you like with a pestle and mortar.
3. To the dough, apply it and mix properly. For at least 30 minutes, let the dough sit in a cool position.
4. Braise the almonds by dumping boiling water over them and making them sit for a few moments while the pastry mixture rests.
5. When the skin quickly falls off, they are prepared. In a mixing bowl, skin all the nuts and grind them into a good meal.
6. Melt butter in a medium bowl and set aside to cool. In a flexible batter, beat the eggs and the sugars and add the almonds, almond flavoring, and butter.
7. When well mixed, stir together. Grease the little tartlet cartons with butter.
8. With a light coating of dough, line the molds and cover them with the nut mixture nearly to the end.
9. Bake at 400°F in the pan for about fifteen minutes. The cakes are expected to have a light golden color on top.
10. Before extracting the cakes from the mold, let them chill a little.
11. Prepare the icing as the cake bakes. Apply the confectioner's sugar to a little container and drip in the fruit juice.
12. The coating over the tarts should be a little dense but also easy to moisten.
13. Before icing them, wait till the tarts have cooled.

2.10 Chocolate Swiss Roll Cake

Cooking Time: 2 hours

Serving Size: 8 to 10

Ingredients:

For the Cake

- ¼ teaspoon table salt
- 2 tablespoons cocoa powder
- 6 large eggs
- ¾ cup of sugar
- 3 tablespoons strong coffee
- 1 cup of chocolate chips

For the Ganache

- ½ cup heavy cream
- 4 ounces of chocolate chips

For the Filling

- ½ teaspoon vanilla extract
- 2 tablespoons powdered sugar
- 1 cup heavy cream

Method:

1. Heat the oven to 350°F. Butter or grease a jellyroll pan.
2. Cover the bottom with a sheet of waxed or linen paper lengthwise.

3. In a thermal bowl and microwave, mix the chocolate and espresso for 45 seconds.
4. Stir and begin to heat until the chocolate is almost molten, in 2-minute bursts.
5. Continue to stir until it has fully melted. Let it cool.
6. Shake the egg yolks until dark and fluffy in the bowl of an immersion blender fitted with a whisk attachment.
7. Add the sugar steadily and begin to beat until the yolks are light and ribbonry.
8. Stir the cooling chocolate into the egg mix softly.
9. Beat egg whites with salts in a small bowl of an immersion blender fitted with the whisk extension until they maintain stiff peaks.
10. To lighten it up, stir a fifth of the egg white solution into the chocolate yolk mixture.
11. In three combinations, softly incorporate the remaining whites into the cake batter.
12. Drop the batter onto the smooth top of the prepared plate. Bake for 15 minutes in an oven and bake for a jelly roll sheet just until the cake layer is dry to the touch.
13. Switch to a baking sheet and cover the top for ten minutes with a lightly soaked towel.
14. Remove the sheets and loop a knife along the cake's sides.
15. Sift over the top of the cake with one teaspoon of cocoa and protect the cake with a thin coffee or flour sack cloth that is a little longer than the plate.
16. Over the cake, sift the leftover tablespoon of cocoa powder. Roll the cake up with the towel

such that the towel is inside, from short end to short end.

17. Beat heavy cream with powder sugar and vanilla until cold, before stiff peaks are preserved.
18. Have your serve plate ready and put it next to your roll of cake. Unroll the chocolate cake softly.
19. Layer the whipped cream filling thinly over the cake, leaving the far edge with a 1-inch margin.
20. To keep its form, wrap the log securely in plastic and place it in the fridge when cooking the ganache.
21. For 45 seconds, microwave the cocoa and icing in a glass container. Stir and begin to heat until molten and flat, in 20-second bursts.
22. Chill for another ten minutes before it thickens.
23. The cake can be kept for up to two days in the fridge in an airtight bag, but the icing can flatten the longer it is stored.

2.11 Summer Berry Tart

Cooking Time: 50 minutes

Serving Size: 8

Ingredients:

- 1 Vanilla bean seeds
- 1 tablespoon rum

- 600g Mixed berries-
- ½ cup Crème Fraiche
- ¼ cup Icing Sugar
- 4 Meringue nests
- 1 cup Double Cream

For the Tart

- Milk- a little splash
- Butter
- Flour 2 cups
- Unsalted butter 4oz.
- Egg-1 large
- Icing sugar ¼ cup

Method:

1. In a big cup, blend the flour and powdered sugar, add cubed butter and work in the combination until it contains coarse crumbs.
2. Just beat the eggs and a little milk to put the dough together and shape it into a ball.
3. Cover it in plastic wrap and place it for 30 minutes in the refrigerator.
4. Spray some flour with the worktop and the rolling pin, take the mixture out of the refrigerator, and roll it out big enough just to match a 9' loose base tart tin.
5. Lubricate the tart tin with some butter, drain the dough over the rolling pin and pass it to the tart tin to ensure that the sides develop.

6. Trim off the excess bits and stab it all over with a spoon, cover it with a cling film and place it back for 30 minutes in the refrigerator.
7. To 350F, heat the oven.
8. Take out the tart mixture from the refrigerator and line it with baking parchment pressing it to the edges; fill the tart with baked beans or grains and bake it for ten minutes, empty it, remove the baking bean and parchment paper and cook until solid and crispy, allow to cool before lining it for ten minutes longer.
9. Whip the double icing and crème Fraiche with powdered sugar, vanilla bean seeds, and rum until soft peaks are formed before serving.
10. Combine it with shattered nests of meringue, and the combination will fill your tart.

2.12 Almond cake

Cooking Time: 1 hour 45 minutes

Serving Size: one 9-inch cake

Ingredients:

Cake

- 1 tablespoon orange zest
- 3 tablespoons orange juice

- 3 ½ ounces butter
- ½ cup all-purpose flour
- 3 tablespoons milk
- ¾ cup blanched almonds
- ½ cup brown sugar
- ½ cup natural cane sugar
- 3 egg whites
- 3 egg yolks

Almond and Caramel Topping

- ¾ cup blanched almonds
- ¼ cup brown sugar
- 3 ½ ounces butter

Method:
1. Heat the oven to 175°C.
2. Lubricate a 9-inch springs pan and scatter generously with some breadcrumbs.
3. In a mixing bowl, process the blanched almond for the cake until finely ground; there may still be little bits of almonds remaining.
4. Soften butter and brown sugar together till well mixed and smooth.
5. Insert one egg yolk at a time and blend properly. Sift in the powder and gently fold it into the batter along with the ground almonds.
6. Mix in the orange zest and cream. Stir as little as possible before you have a batter that is even and moist.

7. Mix the egg white in a grease-free cup with an electronic whisk. Add in the cane sugar bit by bit as soft peaks form.
8. Whisk until they form rigid peaks. Fold the combination of sugar and egg white gently into the batter and keep flipping until the batter is mixed uniformly.
9. Onto the greased and breaded spring shape pan, drop the batter. Be alert not to stir unnecessarily.
10. Bake in the lower portion of the oven for 30 minutes at 350°F. When baking a cake, make the almonds and caramel topping fast.
11. Along with the brown sugar, heat the butter. Meanwhile, the majority of the blanched almonds are finely sliced.
12. Add the almonds and mix while the butter and sugar are melted, before the caramel thickness increases.
13. Remove the cake from the oven. Pour the almonds and caramel over, spread it uniformly and carefully.
14. When put into the thickest section of the cake, bake a cake for the next five to ten minutes or until the cake has a good color.
15. Pick the cake and let it cool in the fridge. Remove the cake from the pan until it has cooled.

2.13 Fava Bean and Radish Bruschetta

Cooking Time: 40 minutes

Serving Size: 8

Ingredients:

Cake

- ¼ cup olive oil
- 1 clove garlic (peeled)
- 1 pound fava beans (shelled)
- Black pepper
- 8 baguette slices
- 3 radishes
- 1 tablespoon fennel fronds
- Salt
- 1 teaspoon lemon zest
- 1 tablespoon lemon juice
- 1 tablespoon mint leaves

Method:

1. Hot pan of salted water to a boil and simmer for two minutes with the fava beans.
2. Drain the beans and move them to a big bowl of ice water. Let it cool and rinse, then.
3. Drop off each bean with the outer skin and dispose of the skin.
4. Place the beans in a wide bowl and mash them coarsely, keeping some beans entire or in pieces with a fork.
5. Integrate the fennel fronds, peas, radishes, lime juice, lemon zest, and mint leaves.

6. Sprinkle with salt to taste.
7. Dust olive oil over the baguette slices on both sides and barbecue or broil.
8. Dust the sandwich with cloves, and then place it on top of the fava bean combination.
9. Sprinkle on top with a touch of extra salt and serve.

2.14 Egg, Arugula and Herb Tartine

Cooking Time: 20 minutes

Serving Size: 1

Ingredients:
- 1 egg
- Salt and pepper
- 2 slices good bread
- Several chives stalk
- 1 tablespoon butter
- 1 sprig tender rosemary
- 2 big handfuls of baby arugula

Method:
1. Toast the bread and brush the butter over it.

2. As the remainder of the butter heats in a small strong sauté pan, loosely cut the herbs and arugula.
3. For just less than a minute, or until mildly wilted, sauté the herbs and leaves.
4. Insert the egg and cook rapidly over medium-high heat until the vegetables are barely cooked.
5. Remove away from the heat.
6. Sprinkle with salt, pour on the toasted bread, and eat right away.

2.15 Swedish Ginger Cookies

Cooking Time: 70 minutes

Serving Size: 9 cookies

Ingredients:
- 1 cup of sugar
- 1 large egg (beaten)

- 3 ½ cups all-purpose flour
- 1 teaspoon orange zest
- 1 cup unsalted butter
- 2 teaspoons ginger
- ½ teaspoon salt
- ½ cup dark corn syrup
- 2 teaspoons cloves
- 1 teaspoon baking soda
- 2 teaspoons cinnamon
- Pearl sugar (for dusting)

Method:
1. Whisk together the rice, garlic, cinnamon, ginger, baking soda, and salts in a big cup.
2. Heat the corn syrup and orange zest in a shallow frying pan over medium heat.
3. Insert the sugar and butter and proceed to warm until molten, stirring regularly.
4. Take off from the heat and let it cool down to room temperature. To mix, beat the eggs and combine.
5. To blend, pour over the powder mixture and stir. Shape the dough into a ball, roll it in plastic wrap in the double layer, and chill throughout the night.
6. In the top and bottom thirds of the oven, place the racks and heat it to 375 ° F.
7. Line 2 wide baking sheets parchment paper, with baking paper mats.

8. Roll out a part of the dough on a thinly floured surface to a thickness of ¾ inch using a floured rolling pin.
9. Trim the dough into ideal forms, such as triangles, circles, flowers, rings, gingerbread man, and Christmas trees, using cookie cutters.
10. Bake, turning the cookies between the top and bottom racks and rotating the baking sheets roughly halfway through baking, seven to eight minutes until the edges start to tan.
11. To ensure they do not get too brown, check the cookies closely.
12. Let the cookies cool for five minutes on a cookie sheet before switching to a wire rack to allow them to cool fully.
13. Keep going and slice out the cookie dough's remainder and place the cookies on cooling baking sheets.

2.16 Smoked Salmon Smørrebrød

Cooking Time: 25 minutes

Serving Size: 4

Ingredients:
Horseradish Sour Cream

- Kosher salt
- Ground pepper
- ½ cup (mashed) potatoes

- 1 teaspoon flat-leaf parsley (chopped)
- 1 teaspoon lemon juice
- ½ cup sour cream
- 1 teaspoon dill (chopped)
- 1 tablespoon horseradish

Assembly
- Kosher salt
- Ground pepper
- 4 slices Danish rye
- 2 tablespoons salmon
- Dill sprigs
- 2 radishes (sliced)
- 8 ounces smoked salmon (sliced)

Method:
1. In a shallow cup, whisk together the potatoes, if using sour cream, horseradish, dill, coriander, and lime juice; add salt and pepper.
2. On toast, spread sour horseradish cream and finish with smoked salmon, roe, radishes, dill, and coriander if using.
3. Include spice seasoning.

Chapter 3: Popular Danish Dishes

3.1 Pickled Herring with Danish Rye Bread

Cooking Time: 45 minutes

Serving Size: 4

Ingredients:
- 4 sprigs of thyme
- 2 chilies (crushed)

- 3 shallots
- ½ teaspoon dill seeds
- Half inch piece of ginger
- 1 teaspoon peppercorn
- 1 teaspoon coriander seeds
- 1 teaspoon allspice
- ½ teaspoon mustard seed
- 400 ml of sugar
- 5 bay leaves
- 600 ml vinegar

Method:
1. Start by getting the marinade prepared.
2. In a steel or enamel-coated bowl, gradually warm the vinegar and sugar.
3. When the sugar is fully dissolved, add the other components and leave for approximately 5 minutes over moderate flame.
4. Take the heat from the fermenting marinade and allow it to cool fully.
5. Dust and fillet the herrings, meantime.
6. Cut off the head with a thin, narrow knife and make a puncture in the stomach. Withdraw the insides.
7. Remove the tail and fins off and create a deep cut around the top of the fish.
8. Carefully take one filet off the fish when operating with your fingertips, then softly pull the backbone off the second filet.

9. To slice out bones and trim off extra skin, use a sharp knife.
10. The method of fermenting softens them so that when consumed, they are not visible.
11. Break the fillets into three or four pieces together.
12. Place in the container the herring bits, rotating between surfaces of fish and onions that are pickled.
13. Cover the container with the liquid for pickling.
14. Put a cover on each container and chill in the fridge before eating for at least 12 hours. In the fridge, the pickled herring will last at least two weeks.
15. Using a few fresh basil pieces and a dill sprig to serve 2-3 bits of herring on toasted Danish rye bread.

3.2 Cured Salmon

Cooking Time: 1 hour + freezing time

Serving Size: 4

Ingredients:
- 1 teaspoon of fennel seed
- 1 teaspoon of black pepper
- 2 kg salmon filet
- 1 teaspoon of ground cumin
- 1 teaspoon of mustard seed
- 5 tablespoon sugar

- 2 large bunches of dill (chopped)
- 2 teaspoon coriander seed
- 5 tablespoon coarse salt

Method:
1. Making sure that a very clean glass casserole dish is plenty large to accommodate the filets.
2. Rinse and clean away any scaling with the salmon filets, then pat it dry with a clean cloth.
3. Place the skin side of the filets flat next to one another.
4. Create the remedy by adding the sugar, salt, and seasoning together.
5. Spread uniformly over one of the salmon fillets with the minced dill.
6. Flip over the other fillet and lay it on top of the dill. In the steel casserole, position the stack of fillets and protect them with plastic wrap.
7. To push down on the filets, put a work surface or other flat item on the top filet, and apply a weight of some sort (like a slab).
8. For three days, put it in the fridge the salmon. Flip the fillets every 12 hours over those 3 days.
9. Break the fillets into multiple sections after three days, wrap them in plastic, and freeze for 24 hours.
10. Take out of the freezer and slice thinly when you want to consume your gravad laks by chopping diagonally through the filet.

3.3 Fish Filet with Dill Crème Fraiche

Cooking Time: 40 minutes

Serving Size: 4 sandwiches

Ingredients:

- 4 slices Danish rye bread
- Lettuce to garnish
- 4 sole fillets
- 1 teaspoon sugar
- Salt to taste
- 4 tablespoon rye flour
- 2 tablespoon pickles (chopped)
- 1 tablespoon lemon juice
- 1 egg
- Butter
- 2 tablespoon parsley (chopped)
- ½ cup crème Fraiche
- 2 tablespoon dill (chopped)

Method:

1. In a cup, blend the crème Fraiche, parsley, dill, lime juice, and honey.
2. To let the flavors come together, put it in the fridge.
3. Whip the egg in a pan.
4. In a cup, add rye flour and season with salt and pepper.

5. Dip the fish fillets in the egg and dredge them with rye flour.
6. Fry pounded fish over medium-high heat in oil until translucent.
7. Remove from the pan and allow it on the paper towel to cool.
8. Cover the lettuce bread with a hot fish filet and a spoonful of sauce.
9. Serve with a slice of lemon and consume with a fork and knife.
10. Enjoy Tuborg with larger wine.

3.4 Danish Liver Paté

Cooking Time: 1 hour 50 minutes

Serving Size: 4-6

Ingredients:
- 6 sprigs thyme
- ¼ teaspoon allspice
- 400g pork (sliced)
- 1 teaspoon salt
- ½ teaspoon pepper
- 1 small white onion, (chopped)
- 4-5 anchovy filets
- 200g pork fat (chopped)
- 2 chicken livers
- 100 ml of milk

- 1 egg
- 1 tablespoon wheat flour
- 200 ml beef broth
- 1 teaspoon butter

Method:

1. Move the liver frequently through the grinding machine using a meat grinder in the finest atmosphere.
2. Grind the pork fat twice, too.
3. To help bind the paté, produce a thickening roux and melt the butter in a small saucepan and add the flour, stir to cover.
4. When boiling, steadily add the broth and then add the cream.
5. Cook softly over medium-low heat until the "batter" is creamy and brown while continuously stirring.
6. Remove from the heat and quit to cool off. Simultaneously, refine the onion, egg, grilled chicken, and seasoning in a food processor or blender until creamy.
7. Incorporate the ground liver, fatty, roux, and mixed components thoroughly.
8. Pour 4-5 tiny aluminum bake pans into the mixture and top each one with a bay leaf.
9. In a wider one, put small baking dishes and fill midway with warm water.
10. Bake for 35-30 minutes in an oven preheated to 350F.
11. Remove the cooked leverpostej and let it cool slightly before using it.

3.5 Tongue Salad

Cooking Time: 25 minutes

Serving Size: 4

Ingredients:

- Juice of 1 lemon
- A pinch of nutmeg
- 1 cup cooked tongue (chopped)
- ½ teaspoon paprika
- 1 egg yolk (boiled)
- 1 tablespoon butter (softened)
- 1 teaspoon Dijon mustard

Instructions:

1. Place the minced tongue aside, and mix all the other ingredients in a large bowl completely.
2. To mix, add the tongues and mix.
3. For extra crunch, serve two spoonful of tongue salads on a piece of buttered Danish rye bread with onions strips! Enjoy it with the knife and fork!

3.6 Brunette Kartofler

Cooking Time: 20 minutes

Serving Size: 4-6

Ingredients:

- 125g sugar
- 8 tablespoons butter (melted)
- 750g small potatoes (cooked)

Instructions:
1. Melt the sugars in a large skillet over medium heat.
2. Leave for several minutes to cook before it becomes golden brown.
3. Stir in the molten butter.
4. Add vegetables. You will have to move them, not so many at a time.
5. Stir constantly until the caramel is uniformly mixed with the potatoes.
6. Place them in a preheated roasting tray and continue until you have finished all the potatoes.

3.7 Fried Pork And Parsley Sauce

Cooking Time: 120 minutes

Serving Size: 4-6

Ingredients:
- Salt
- Pepper
- 1000g pork belly (unsalted)

- 2 dl parsley
- ¼ teaspoon nutmeg
- 1 kg of potatoes
- 4 dl milk
- 1 dl whipping cream
- 50g Danish butter
- 4 tablespoons wheat flour

Instructions:

1. Break the pork belly into slices 5 with a thickness of 6 mm, then dry the cuts for a while on the cling film towel.
2. Before cooking, sprinkle the pieces with salt and black pepper.
3. Begin to peel the potatoes. Place them in a saucepan and cover with cold water.
4. For 15 minutes, steam the potatoes. If you like, you should keep the skin on it. Especially the "new" seasonal potatoes with very small, tender white skin.
5. Cut the parsley into bits. Create a butterball of butter and starch and constantly stir until the combination is turned into a uniform mass when melting in the saucepot.
6. Add the milk and mix. Repeat until you like the sauce with the consistency you want. Not too dense and not too thin.
7. Do not cook the gravy. A kind of white "béchamel sauce" will end up.
8. Stir in the whipped cream, then taste the sauce.

9. Put in nutmeg - if you like. Then insert all the chopped parsley when mixing - and add salt and pepper to taste.

10. Let the sauce boil for ten minutes while soaking up the flavor - so the components are blended and stirred together.

11. On either side of a hot pan, cook the pulled pork sliced for almost two minutes with medium heat until they seem crisp and with a translucent surface.

12. In the heated 200°F oven, place the pork belly and roast for 20 minutes - thus rotating the slices after quarter reheating time.

13. It is easier to barbecue the pork belly strips on a well-heated camping stove in the summertime.

14. Place on a warm surface the lukewarm potato and place the crispy pork belly pieces, then spill over the potato the hot and dry parsley sauce.

15. Toss the dish with some fresh minced parsley and eat.

3.8 Danish Rice Dessert

Cooking Time: 90 minutes

Serving Size: 4

Ingredients:

Rice Pudding

- 1-liter milk
- 2 vanilla beans

- 1 dl water
- 2.25 dl white rice

Risalamande

- 5 dl heavy cream
- One can cherry sauce (for topping)
- 2 tablespoon sugar
- 150 g almonds

Instructions:

1. Transfer the rice and water to a saucepan. Warm it up and let it simmer for two minutes or so.
2. Transfer the milk to the mixture and cook until it boils, stirring continuously.
3. Add the vanilla bean pods. This is accomplished by cutting the vanilla beans by using a knife to scrape out the pods.
4. Use two tablespoons of sugar to incorporate the vanilla. Additionally, add to the mixture the hollow vanilla beans.
5. Let the pudding boil at low temperatures under the cover. The rice continues to burn in the saucepan, so don't forget to stir periodically.
6. For about 35 minutes, let it boil.
7. Take the empty vanilla beans. Now the rice pudding is finished.
8. Before continuing to make the Risalamande, let it chill in the refrigerator. You can prepare this rice pudding the first day in advance.
9. Heat the water and pour it into a shallow saucepan until the boiling point.

10. For around 5-7 minutes, add the nuts and let them sit in the warm water.
11. The almonds are picked up one-by-one and squeezed middle finger so that the peel extracts from the almond. When required, add more hot water.
12. Skinning almonds should be simple. Cut the almonds thinly sliced and blend them with the cool rice pudding.
13. Add it to the dessert with cold rice and blend properly.
14. In a separate pan, mix the heavy cream into whipped cream and mix gently with the rice pudding.
15. The Risalamande has now been completed. On serving, place it in the refrigerator.

3.9 Danish Meatballs

Cooking Time: 65 minutes

Serving Size: 6

Ingredients:

- Salt and pepper to taste
- ¼ cup margarine
- ¼ cup all-purpose flour
- ¼ cup seltzer water
- ½ pound veal
- 1 egg
- ¼ cup bread crumbs
- ½ pound pork
- ¼ cup onion
- ¼ cup milk

Instructions:

1. In a dish, mix all the veal and pork and whisk in the milk, cabbage, and egg.
2. Add the crumbs of the bread to the beef. Sprinkle with the flour and squeeze to mix properly.
3. Stir in the water from the seltzer, sprinkle with salt and black pepper and, blend properly.
4. The blend should be very sticky, but it should not spill.
5. In the fridge, chill the leftover marinade for 30 minutes to make the meatballs easier to mold.
6. Heat the margarine over moderate heat in a large pan.

7. Scoop up roughly 2½ tablespoons of cooking liquid with a large spoon to shape meatballs, and form the combination into a slightly compressed, circular meatball about the size of an average egg.

Put the meatballs into the heated pan, and fry for around fifteen minutes per hand, until the meatballs are well-browned and no longer pink in the middle

3.10 Danish Roast Pork With Cracking

Cooking Time: 105 minutes

Serving Size: 5

Ingredients:

- coarse salt
- 5 dried bay leaves
- 1kg Boneless pork roast

Instructions:

1. To carve long, deep grooves in the crust of the pork roast, use a paring blade.
2. The grooves can have a separation of around 5 mm (half an inch).
3. Make sure that the rind has deep grooves, but do not hack through the real beef.
4. Clean the whole roast with coarse sea salt deeply. Make sure you get a lot of salt from the grooves.
5. In the grooves, position 3-6 dried bay leaf - if you would not have any, this can be skipped.
6. On a shelf with a baking dish underneath, put the roast.

7. Put two cups (half a liter) of water and some diced onions and carrots in the roasting pan. This water will later be used on the veggies to make a good gravy.
8. Be sure that in a normal direction, the roast is sitting. To level it, you should use a ball of aluminum foil beneath the roast.
9. If you are not doing this, you risk having an inconsistent color or burning the rind. Heat the oven to 440 F and let the roast cook for fifteen minutes.
10. Switch down the temperature to 400 F and begin to cook.
11. Switch on the grill option in the oven when the temperature is 57C. This means that the rind will be fresh and crisp.
12. Keep an eye on your roast because you're not going to burn it.
13. When the temperature is 65C, the roast is cooked at 150 F. To attain this level, and it takes about 50 minutes. You should add a little extra if the water evaporates while cooking.
14. Take it out of the oven when the roasting is finished. Let it rest for about fifteen minutes or quickly eat it.
15. Drain the vegetables from the water and dump them into a saucepan if you want to make a good gravy.
16. Apply some heavy cream and some coloring with brown gravy. To taste, apply salt.

3.11 Danish Cold Buttermilk Soup

Cooking Time: 15 minutes

Serving Size: 5

Ingredients:

- 1 tablespoon sugar
- 1 tablespoon lemon juice
- 2 tablespoon cane sugar
- 1 vanilla bean
- 4 egg yolks
- 1-liter buttermilk
- 1-liter plain yogurt

Instructions:

1. Mix the yolks and sugars into a soft and airy mixture using a hand mixer.
2. From a vanilla bean, pick the vanilla seeds out.
3. Use one tablespoon of sugar to combine the vanilla seeds.
4. Along with the yolks, stir the vanilla bean.
5. Stir the egg yolks with the yogurt. Add four steps of the yogurt and shake well in between each phase.
6. Eventually, add the buttermilk and blend it well. Add lime juice flavoring.
7. Leave the soup in the fridge with the buttermilk.
8. The unused vanilla beans should be left in the cup as they still have a lot of wonderful taste.

3.12 Danish Breaded Pork Patties

Cooking Time: 30 minutes

Serving Size: 2-3

Ingredients:

- Salt and pepper
- 50g of butter
- 2 tablespoon water
- 70g bread crumbs
- 1 egg
- 500g ground pork

Instructions:

1. Begin by splitting the meat into five pieces of approximately 100 g total and turning them into dense circular patties.
2. Beat the egg and the water on a deep pan.
3. Mix the bread crumbs along with pepper and salt on a second pan.
4. Now, in the beaten egg, roll the pork patties and then in the breadcrumbs.
5. Be sure the breadcrumbs surround the whole patty.
6. One time should be adequate, but if you want a thicker breading sheet, repeat this move once again.
7. Transfer the butter to the frying pan and cook the breaded pork patties for around 5 minutes.
8. Switch them over from moment to moment.

3.13 Danish Red Berry Pudding

Cooking Time: 1 hour 15 minutes

Serving Size: 5

Ingredients:

- 2.5 dl water
- 2 tablespoon potato starch
- 125g strawberry
- 125g sugar
- 1 teaspoon vanilla extract
- 125g blackcurrant
- 125g redcurrant
- 125g raspberry

Instructions:

1. When you are using fresh berries, begin by using cold water to rinse and clean them.
2. Cut in on lower rates for raspberries and strawberries.
3. Move all of the ingredients into a frying pan except the potato starch.
4. Mix all the ingredients and let the berries sit for about an hour in the sweet liquid.
5. Use medium-high heat to heat the combination of berry and water until it boils.
6. For eight minutes, let the solution boil.

7. Turn the heat down and add the cornflour that has been dissolved.
8. Let the red berry pudding boil for an extra five minutes, and stop boiling the mixture.
9. Until serving with cold heavy cream, spill the pudding into 3-4 dishes and let it chill off.
10. Sour cream combined with some vanilla seed is a substitute for heavy cream.

3.14 Danish Apple Cake

Preparation time: 45 minutes

Serving Size: 6-8

Ingredients:
- 300ml whipping cream
- 1 tablespoon plain chocolate
- 500g Brimley apples
- 200g rolled oats
- 125g granulated sugar
- 500g dessert apples
- 2 teaspoon vanilla sugar
- 50g butter
- 3 tablespoon sugar

Instructions:
1. Fill the water in a big jar.

2. Peel, center, and dice the apples thinly and lower them into the water.

3. Drain the water and leave one tablespoon of stewed apples with two tablespoons of sugar and powdered sugar under the cover until tender. (Approximately ten to twenty minutes).

4. Transfer to a bowl of baked apple slices and let settle.

5. Melt the butter over light heat in a large deep fryer, add 125g of sugar, and mix with a spoon.

6. Mix in the grains until they are crispy and buttered once the sugar has turned into caramel with butter (this will take a couple of minutes).

7. (Be careful, so you do not burn). Enable for cooling.

8. Finally, whisk the cream and put half the apple combination in a cup, followed by half the buttered grains, then add a cream layer and customize with rubbed chocolate.

9. Serve right away or until necessary, chill.

3.15 Danish Chicken Tartlet

Cooking Time: 50 minutes

Serving Size: 4

Ingredients:

- 400-gram white asparagus
- Tartlet shells
- 500-gram meat
- 70-gram butter

- 4 tablespoons of flour
- 2 dl Chicken stock
- 2 dl milk
- 1.5-liter water

Instructions:
1. The water should be boiling, and the stock applied.
2. Insert the meat from the hen or poultry and simmer for 20 minutes.
3. Let the chicken over and cut it into tiny chunks, preferably little triangles,
4. Save the fried chicken water.
5. Cook once soft and sliced if fresh asparagus is used.
6. When the butter has melted, take a casserole dish and add butter and starch.
7. Transfer the milk and some boiled chicken water to the mixture.
8. Add a pinch of salt to the sauces and allow for a few minutes to boil.
9. Add the chicken and asparagus to the pan to make sure it is hot.
10. It is time to fill up the tartlets then. Chop parsley and seasoning on top of the tartlets when completed.

3.16 Danish Rye Bread

Cooking Time: 12 hours 25 minutes

Serving Size: 2 bread

Ingredients:

- 1 tablespoon salt
- 2 tablespoon gravy browning
- 2 dl rye kernels
- 4 dl all-purpose flour
- 4 dl rye flour
- 2 dl wheat
- 4 dl sourdough
- 8 dl water
- 2 dl flax seed
- 1 tablespoon malt syrup
- 2 dl sunflower seeds

Instructions:

1. Put the crushed rye kernels, broken wheat, flaxseed, sunflower seeds, water, malt syrup, and sticky dough into a large bucket.
2. Enable all to soak for at least eight hours. This can be achieved in the evenings with benefit so that you can begin the next morning.
3. Insert the remaining ingredients after about eight hours and allow the rye bread dough to rise for about 45 minutes.
4. Cut the mixture into two pieces and dump it into two ordinary pans of bread.
5. With plastic tape, coat the bread pans with.
6. For around 1-2 hours, let the bread rise or the dough pan is full of bread.

7. Bake the rye bread for around 1 hour at 180C.
8. Take the bread from the bread pots and let them cool off until finished.
9. Hold them in an air-tight jar or a plastic bag while the bread is cooled down.

3.17 Danish Meatloaf

Cooking Time: 60 minutes

Serving Size: 4-6

Ingredients:

- Salt and pepper
- 1 pack of bacon
- 1 pound ground pork
- 2 eggs
- 2 tablespoons plain breadcrumbs
- 1 pound ground beef

Sauce

- salt
- milk and all-purpose flour
- 1 cup milk
- a few drops gravy browning
- 2-3 teaspoons redcurrant jelly

Instructions:

1. Sauté the onions and green pepper for five minutes in the butter.

2. Transfer the hot sauce and water to ¼ cup and simmer for another 3 minutes.
3. In a 9x5x3 loaf tray, press the onion mixture onto the rim.
4. Mix the rest of the ingredients and press the onion mixture evenly.
5. Bake for 1 hour at 375°F.
6. Invert the meatloaf on a plate before serving so that the onion/pepper combination is on top.
7. Mix all ingredients of the sauce and cook until thickens. Serve with meatloaf.

Chapter 4: Iceland Food Recipes

4.1 Prawn Paella

Cooking Time: 40 minutes

Serving Size: 4

Ingredients:

- 375g of Iceland king prawns
- 1 tablespoon of Iceland coriander
- 6 bags Iceland golden savory rice
- 1 tablespoon olive oil
- 1 large Iceland onion
- 1 tablespoon Iceland garlic

To Serve

- Lemon wedges

Instructions:

1. In the oil, fry garlic and onion over medium-high heat until they become softer and begin to color. It should be finished in five minutes.
2. Transfer the frozen prawns to the dish and swirl to coat in the mixture until they are nearly defrosted, frying for five minutes, stirring regularly.
3. Add 4-6 sachets of frozen gold rice plus cilantro.
4. To mix, whisk gently.
5. Serve with chopped parsley on the plate.

4.2 Beef And Roasted Veg Lasagna

Cooking Time: 60 minutes

Serving Size: 4

Ingredients:

- About 12 lasagna sheets
- Large handful of mozzarella
- 1 tablespoon olive oil
- Jar of tomato sauce
- Jar of white sauce
- A small handful of Iceland onions
- 1 tablespoon Iceland garlic
- ½ packet of roasted vegetables
- A whole packet of steak mince

To Serve

- Garlic bread
- Salad

Instructions:

1. Heat up to 180C oven.
2. Sauté the garlic and onions in the oil until they soften. Stir in the mince, then fry until browned.
3. Until it's cooked, add vegetables. When you have picky eaters, remove and chop some very big vegetables.
4. Tip into a tomato saucepot, bring to a boil, and cook for 20 minutes.

5. Get the bakery dish and layer it up! Start with a meat sauces layer, then a pasta line (lasagna sheets-use 4-7 in one layer and split up if necessary). There's a layer of cheese sauce now. Then repeat, depending on how large your dishes are, once or several more.
6. Complete the layering with spaghetti, then white sauce, and then apply a generous layer of diced mozzarella to the end. Place it in the oven.
7. When it's heating, pop in your garlic bread at the end and prepare your salad.
8. Bake for 40 minutes until the spaghetti is cooked through and crispy and boiling. Stick a toothpick in the middle to ensure the pasta is good and fluffy all the way around.
9. Serve with salads and toast with garlic

4.3 Beef Enchiladas

Cooking Time: 50 minutes

Serving Size: 4

Ingredients:
- 1 tablespoon chili (chopped)
- Drizzle extra virgin olive oil
- 8 soft tortillas
- 2 large handfuls of cheddar
- 1 tin tomatoes
- 1 tablespoon frozen coriander (chopped)
- 1 tablespoon olive oil
- A small handful of frozen onions (chopped)
- 1 packet of chili spice mix

- 1 jar of kidney beans
- 1 tablespoon frozen garlic (chopped)
- ½ packet of mixed peppers (sliced)
- A whole packet of beef mince

To Serve
- 1 tablespoon chili
- Side salad
- A handful of avocado chunks
- 1 tablespoon of coriander
- Dollops sour cream

Instructions:
1. Defrost the avocado several hours in advance.
2. Heat the oven to 180C.
3. Sauté the garlic and onions in the oil until soft. Stir in the mince and simmer until it's colored.
4. Top in the pepper and seasoning blend and stir constantly.
5. Soak beans, tinned toms, and cilantro now tap in. Let it boil gently with the lid off for 20 minutes.
6. Find a huge baking dish and a breadboard.
7. Place 1 wrapper on the board and spoon down the center of the meat combination.
8. Wrap it and pass it to the baking bowl, making sure it is beneath the tucked in a bit to not unravel. For seven more, do the same.
9. Over the end, grate tons of cheddar and scatter chili on too. Drizzle some extra virgin olive oil with it.

10. Pop it in the oven and simmer for 25 minutes.
11. Make your guacamole by just thoroughly mixing your avocado with cilantro, chili, and coriander.
12. Serve with a spoonful of sour cream, guacamole, and lettuce (or creme fraiche dip).

4.4 Fish Finger Pie

Cooking Time: 25 minutes

Serving Size: 4

Ingredients:

- 1 packet of mashed potato
- Large handful mild cheddar
- 2 tins of baked beans
- 10 fish fingers

To Serve

- 1 packet of tender stem broccoli

Instructions:

1. Heat the oven to 180C.
2. Get a squared dish for baking. Pour the beans down. Lay on top of the fish fingers.
3. For three minutes, microwave your mix.
4. For another two minutes, mix and prepare.
5. To the sandwich, add a coat of mash and sprinkle on tons of grated cheese.
6. For 20 minutes, roast.

7. For three minutes, boil the broccoli. Mix and serve.

8. Try to transfer a spoonful of curry powder or Barbecue sauce to the beans.

4.5 Kuromame Sweetened Black Soybean

Cooking Time: 30 minutes

Serving Size: 4

Ingredients:

- ½ iceberg lettuce
- 4 burger buns
- 4 mini chicken fillets
- 4 tablespoon mayonnaise
- ½ jar pesto

Options to Stack

- 2 tomatoes (sliced)
- 4 Onion rings
- 4 Hash browns

To Serve

- Iceland Corn on the cob
- Iceland sweet potato fries

Instructions:

1. Remove across all packages 4 mini chicken fillets, put on a plate with plastic wrap.

2. Defrost for 13 hours in a freezer.
3. Preheat the oven to 200C.
4. Pop in your 20-minute hash browns and potato wedges, then four minutes later, your onion rings for 16 minutes. Keep an eye on the one minute earlier.
5. In a bowl, ferment the pesto and mix the chicken fillets with pesto to coat them.
6. In a saucepan, heat the oil until warm and fry the fillets for about fifteen minutes, rotating once. Pop the corn for five minutes on the cob in the microwave.
7. Get each burger bun divided. Pop it under the barbecue or in the toaster.
8. Take out the buns and drench the bottom with a touch of extra pesto.
9. Insert the chicken breast, a little chopped lettuce, and then drop some mayo into the top piece. Then pop it on, or line it up.
10. To end, pop a brown hash underneath the chicken, an onion ring on top of the salad, and then a sliced tomato.
11. Serve on the corn with sweet potato chips and corn.

4.6 Superboost Smoothie

Cooking Time: 3 minutes

Serving Size: 4

Ingredients:
- Splash orange juice
- Splash water
- Handful of strawberry
- Handful spinach
- Handful banana

Instructions:
1. Put in a handful of mixed berries and bananas.
2. Put a couple of spinach nuggets.
3. Drop a shot of juice and transfer water to the top.
4. To beautify, reserve a few strawberries.

4.7 Beef Chili Nachos

Cooking Time: 10 minutes
Serving Size: 12

Ingredients:
- Handfuls cheddar cheese
- Handful of avocados
- 1 tablespoon olive oil
- 1 tin of kidney beans
- Tortilla chips
- 475g bag steak mince
- 1 handful onions
- 1 stock cube

- 1 tin tomatoes
- 1 tablespoon garlic
- 1 packet of chili mix con Carne
- 1 teaspoon chili

To Serve

- Dollops of sour cream dip

Instructions:

1. In the butter, fry the onions and garlic for five minutes or until softened.
2. Insert the mince and fry until it is no longer frozen. It could take 5 to 10 more minutes.
3. For the last couple of minutes, top in the stock cube plus the spice mixture.
4. Transfer tanned tomatoes and soaked kidney beans.
5. Turn the heat on and cook with no cover for fifteen minutes, causing most of the liquid to disappear.
6. Now put some tortilla chips on a cookie dish or wide baking sheet, then blot mouthful of the beef chili plus the sauce, the preserved avocado, some cheese and then replicate again: a coating of tortilla chips, then dot over the beef pepper, hot sauce, avocado, and loads of cheese.
7. Pop it for fifteen min under a hot pan. Keep an eye out, as this will capture you quickly.
8. Offer with spoonful of sour cream dip at the center of the table and encourage others.

9. If you like this super spicy, at the vegetables and garlic level, simply add a lot more frozen pepper to the combination.

3.8 Berry Crumble

Cooking Time: 30 minutes

Serving Size: 4

Ingredients:

- 100g plain flour
- 4 tablespoon sugar
- 1 tablespoon brown sugar
- 50g cold butter cubes
- 1 bag of berries

Instructions:

1. Preheat the oven to 180C. Add a spoonful of sugar to combine.
2. Scatter frozen fruit into a cookie sheet.
3. Rub the starch into the butter until it feels like breadcrumbs, and lightly rub.
4. Mix in the sugar now.
5. Cover the fruit with a sprinkle topping.
6. Spray a little additional sugar on top and bake for about thirty minutes or until the fruit is bubbling and it's baked through and caramelized on top.
7. With custard or milk, prepare.
8. Try this in the mixture of sliced apples, too. Orbits of rhubarb.

4.9 Super Veg Cottage Pie

Cooking Time: 60 minutes

Serving Size: 4

Ingredients:

- 1 packet of carrot and mash sweet potato
- Handful of cheddar
- 1 tablespoon olive oil
- 1 beef stock cube
- A handful of mixed vegetables
- 1 tin of tomatoes
- 1 tablespoon of mixed herbs
- Whole packet beef mince
- Small handful onions
- 1 tablespoon garlic

Serve

- Cabbage
- Gravy

Instructions:

1. Heat the oven to 180C.
2. Sauté in oil with onions and garlic. Insert beef mince when defrosted and fry until golden.
3. Insert the vegetables and whisk until the mixture is defrosted.
4. Now add the bucket of stock, the fresh basil, and the tomatoes.

5. Bring it to a boil and cook for 20 minutes.
6. As per packet directions, microwave your carrot mash and sweet potato.
7. In a baking bowl, pop the beef mixture and cover it with the mash.
8. Insert lots of cheese and cook until crispy and bubbling, for 30-40 minutes.
9. Tear a cabbage and pour some hot water over it for ten minutes until it is supposed to come out and cook with a cover.
10. Toss in the sugar, salt, and black pepper, then rinse. Make the gravy.
11. Serve the gravy and vegetable pie.

4.10 Superboost Soup

Cooking Time: 40 minutes

Serving Size: 4

Ingredients:
- 1 stockpot
- 1 tablespoon coriander
- ⅔ bag floret and carrot mix
- ¼ bag frozen spinach
- 1 teaspoon ginger
- 1 teaspoon chili
- 1 tablespoon olive oil
- 1 tablespoon garlic
- Handful onions

Instructions:
1. Sauté in oil with onions, garlic, chili, and spice.
2. To cover the vegetables, add floret and carrot mixture and ample made-up stocks.
3. Simmer until it becomes soft. Near the top, insert spinach for about ten minutes before it splits and can be blended in.
4. Whizz the soup until creamy and nice. If required, include a little boiling water to release it.
5. Right into the spicy broth, add cilantro.
6. Do not add too many stocks in because it is much harder to soften if you bring in too much.
7. When using beef stock or bowls, don't sprinkle with salt as they are always salty.

4.11 Beefy Baked Bean Pie

Cooking Time: 45 minutes

Serving Size: 4

Ingredients:
- Iceland frozen mash
- Grated Iceland mild cheddar
- 1 tablespoon olive oil
- 1 beef stock cube

- A little pepper
- Small handful onions
- 2 tins of baked beans
- A whole packet of beef mince

To Serve
- Jug of gravy
- Iceland petit poi's

Instructions:
1. Heat the oven to 180C.
2. In the butter, soften the onions.
3. In the grill, add the meat and defrost, and cook until golden.
4. Insert a stock cube and a bit of water (half of the total of a mug) and get it to boil.
5. Carry the beans to 2 tins. Take it to a boil and cook for fifteen minutes.
6. With some spice, season.
7. Microwave the pie with enough mash to coat it.
8. Pour it into a bowl for cooking.
9. Cover with mash and a lot of grated cheese afterward. For 20 minutes, roast.
10. Serve with the beans and a mug of gravy made and use the box instructions.
11. Try this in place of mince or sausages. Simply cook the frozen sausage rolls for 15 minutes and cut the onions and garlic.

4.12 Tasty Chicken Curry

Cooking Time: 50 minutes

Serving Size: 4

Ingredients:

- 1 handful of spinach
- 1 handful of fine green beans
- 1 tablespoon vegetable oil
- 1 jar of mild curry sauce
- A small handful of coriander
- Small handful onions
- 1 tablespoon chili
- ½ a packet of mini chicken fillets
- 1 tablespoon garlic
- 1 tablespoon ginger

To Serve

- 2 packets of Plain naan bread
- 4 bags of white rice

Instructions:

1. In oil, cook the onion, ginger, garlic, and chili.
2. Insert the mini chicken fillets and fry until nearly cooked and no more frozen.
3. Chop them in two with a set of clean blades if you find them too big for your family.
4. Insert the curry sauce, put it to a boil, and cook for fifteen minutes.

5. Include the spinach after four minutes. Stir to melt when it defrosts.
6. Seven minutes until you are about to eat, add cilantro and green beans. Occasionally swirl.
7. In the oven, cook the naan bun and heat the rice.
8. Whatever you want, add extra chili. Get it colder by choosing a cooler sauce container.

4.13 Secret Ingredient Chocolate Cake

Cooking Time: 40 minutes

Serving Size: 4+

Ingredients:

- 1 teaspoon baking powder
- 1 large egg
- 150g dark chocolate
- 900g ¼ bag of mashed potato
- 100g sugar
- 200g self-rising flour
- 100g condensed milk

Milk Chocolate Icing

- 20g block butter
- 150g condensed milk
- 150g milk chocolate

Instructions:

1. The night ahead, defrost the mash in the freezer.

2. Heat the oven to 180C.
3. Over a pan of boiling water, pop a heatproof mug. Do not let the water hit the bowl.
4. Melt the broken bar of chocolate in a pan. Insert condensed milk, butter, and sugar. Gently blend as it is melting.
5. Remove from the heat and enable to cool down slightly.
6. In a pan, season the flour and mixing powder, transfer the mash to the pot, and mix the chocolate combination.
7. Shake and add the egg, too. Mix thoroughly.
8. Grease and cover with greaseproof paper 20cm loosely bottom sandwich muffin tins.
9. Transfer the blend to the tins, separating evenly.
10. Roast it for thirty minutes. Do the icing in the meantime.
11. Like the above, melt the cookies, condensed butter, and milk. Just allow it to cool.
12. Enable the cakes in their tins to cool slowly, then extract them from the tins and enable them to cool entirely.
13. For the coloring, sandwich the cakes together. Then top this all over the edges with some too-smother.
14. Customize the buttons with cocoa powder.

4.14 Cheat's Berry Brulee

Cooking Time: 15 minutes

Serving Size: 4

Ingredients:

- 1 pack of custard
- Brown sugar on top
- 2 tablespoon sugar
- Half a pack of different berries

Instructions:

1. To make a puree, boil the frozen fruit with two tablespoons of sugar.
2. Fill four heatproof compote saucepans with ¾ of them.
3. As directed, heat the custard in the microwave.
4. Put a nice sprinkle of brown sugar on top and load each ramekin with hot custard.
5. Pop it under a hot pan until it fills with honey.
6. A blow torch is an ideal way for the same result to be done! But if you do not have one, it is just fine with the grill.

4.15 Sunday Roast

Cooking Time: 90 minutes

Serving Size: 4

Ingredients:

- Lamb leg with mint sauce

Vegetables

- Goose fat roast potatoes
- Carrot swede mash

- Cauliflower Broc cheese

Extras

- Sage and Onion stuffing balls
- Yorkshire puddings

To Serve

- Gravy

Instructions:

1. Heat the oven to 180C.
2. Pop in your meat and cook, as instructed, 1 hour and five minutes for the lamb.
3. Place the caulis Broc cheese first, the roast potato next for 35 minutes, the stuffing balls after 25 minutes, and then Yorkshire puddings.
4. Microwave the frozen carrot swede smash.
5. As per packet instructions, let the gravy continue.
6. Have a note of when you intend to eat and go out, and remember how long it takes each part to go into the oven and where it has to go.
7. In the sauce, a little splash of red wine will make it taste handmade.

4.16 Fruity Cakes

Cooking Time: 30 minutes

Serving Size: 12

Ingredients:

- 1 teaspoon baking powder

- Large handful blueberries
- 300g self-rising flour
- 140ml milk
- 100g caster sugar
- 2 large eggs
- 100g butter

Instructions:
1. In a muffin pan, heat oven 180 and pop-paper baking cases.
2. Mix ambient temperature butter and sugars until well combined, then one at the moment, add an egg.
3. Incorporate flour and baking powder.
4. When combined, add the milk in gradually while introducing blueberries.
5. Blend pop into cake lining.
6. Bake until well rose and crispy, for 15-20 minutes.
7. Cool for ten minutes in a tray before the withdrawal.
8. Place a little water (or lime juice) with a few teaspoons of powdered sugar and sprinkle.
9. Drizzle the runny paste over the chilled, fruity cakes.

4.16 Bangers And Cheesy Mustard Mash

Cooking Time: 45 minutes

Serving Size: 4

Ingredients:

- 3 red onions (sliced)
- Gravy
- 8-10 sausages
- 1 knob of butter
- 1 tablespoon oil
- 1 packet of grated cheddar cheese
- 1 packet of mash

To Serve

- 1 bowl of peas

Instructions:

1. Heat the oven to 180C.
2. Cook the sausages for 30 minutes in the oven.
3. Fry the sliced spring onions until tender, around ten minutes, in a little oil.
4. In the meantime, according to the guidance, microwave mash for five minutes.
5. Then add a bit of butter and melted butter.
6. Shake for a further thirty seconds and heat so that the cheese melts.
7. Create gravy with hot water, remove the onions from the heat, and add gravy into the combination of onions and whisk thoroughly.
8. In the oven, roast your peas. Offer with the sausages, scramble, and plenty of caramelized onions alongside.

4.17 Chicken Pesto Tart

Cooking Time: 30 minutes

Serving Size: 4

Ingredients:

- Large handful mozzarella
- A handful of cherry tomatoes
- 1 block of puff pastry
- Jar of pesto Russo
- ½ packet of chicken strips

To Serve

- Salad
- Butter
- Baby Potatoes

Instructions:

1. Defrost the pastry overnight, as directed.
2. Remove from the refrigerator as per the directions before use.
3. Heat the oven to 180C.
4. Roll out the pie into a straight elongated and mark a 1.5-centimeter margin along the pie's edge using a paring blade.
5. This will create the borders of your tart.
6. Strangle the pesto, but leave the pesto in the square that you have created.
7. Shake over the strips of chicken.

8. Now add a couple of cherry tomatoes that are halved.
9. The next top has plenty of rubbed mozzarella.
10. Bake until fried and boiling, or 25 minutes.
11. Serve with a tray of fresh peas, butter on top, and a side dish.
12. Drizzle with extra virgin olive oil for warmth and flavor just before baking.

4.18 Friday Night Kebabs

Cooking Time: 30 minutes

Serving Size: 4

Ingredients:
- Garlic sauce
- Chilli sauce
- 2 packets of meatballs
- Handful Romaine lettuce
- Iceland tomatoes
- Handful onions
- 4 Iceland pittas

Instructions:
1. Heat the oven to 180C.
2. Cook the meatballs for thirty minutes.

3. Value the edge of your pitta bread partly before baking, as this makes opening your pitta even smoother after baking it. Toast your Pitta gently.
4. By carefully pressing in a knife, wrench it open but make sure it remains intact.
5. Cover with one or two meatballs and lots of garlic, then add cabbage, tomato, onion, chili sauce, and jalapenos.
6. For a better and more natural version, use unsweetened yogurt with grated cloves instead of sauce.

Chapter 5: Traditional Vikings Recipes

5.1 Ballyvolane Gravadlax with Cucumber Pickle

Cooking Time: 30 minutes

Serving Size: 8

Ingredients:
- 2 tablespoon black pepper
- 4 tablespoon fresh dill
- 2 tablespoon of sea salt
- 2 tablespoon sugar
- 900g 2 sides of salmon

For the Dill Mustard Mayonnaise

- 1 tablespoon of dill
- Salt and pepper
- 1 large egg yolk
- ½ pint of sunflower oil
- 1tablespoon of wine vinegar
- 1 tablespoon of white sugar
- 2 tablespoons of French mustard

For the Cucumber Pickle

- 1 small shallot
- 3 tablespoon hot water
- 1 cucumber
- 1 tablespoon salt
- 1 small red chili
- 4 tablespoon caster sugar
- 4 tablespoon rice vinegar
-

Instructions:

1. Mix in the cinnamon, sugar, spice, and dill.
2. Place one side of the fish on the cling film and scatter it on the solution to ensure that it is covered uniformly.
3. Cover this prepared portion with salmon on the other hand.
4. In the cling film, seal all the fish well and chill in the fridge. Turn it on for four days. On day 5, it will be set.
5. Break the cucumber lengthwise in half.

6. Slice rather finely, ideally if you have one, using the thinnest configuration of a mandolin.
7. Incorporate the sugar, spice, vinegar, and warm water in a bowl until mixed, then add the cucumber, parsley, and red chili.
8. Move to individual serving containers and put before serving to refrigerate overnight.
9. In a mug, mix the yolk, mustard, and sugar slowly until mixed.
10. When the solution has emulsified, incorporate the oil drop at a time, then add the vinegar and dill. With salt and black pepper, spray.

5.2 Chopped Steak with Mushroom and Bacon Gravy

Cooking Time: 50 minutes

Serving Size: 4-6

Ingredients:
- 1 tablespoon thyme leaves
- Salt and fresh (cracked) pepper
- ½ Pound bacon mine was smoked
- ½ cup beef broth
- 1 tablespoon Worcestershire sauce
- 1 ½ pound beef ground sirloin
- ½ medium onion (chopped)
- 2 cloves garlic (smashed)

- ½ cup heavy cream
- 8 ounces cremini mushrooms
- ½ ounce package wild mushrooms

Instructions:

1. To a simmer, warm the cream and then insert the dried mushrooms.
2. Stir in cream to coat them, and then let sit for thirty minutes.
3. Cook the bacon and put on hand towels until crispy.
4. Give a moderate chop to the bacon, reserving 4 bits for your burger to edge.
5. Drain all but two tablespoons of oil from the pot and cook it again over medium-high flame. On both ends, brown the burgers nicely.
6. To the pan, transfer a stick of butter and a tablespoon of olive oil and sauté the fresh mushrooms, onion, and cloves for a few minutes until the onions are tender and the mushrooms begin to brown.
7. Add the broth to make sure all browned pieces from the pan are scraped off.
8. Insert the thyme, Worcestershire sauce, the mushrooms, and their cream to soak. Sprinkle with salt to taste.
9. Dip the sauce back into the burger, turn heat low, and cook till the burgers are finished.
10. Garnish each burger with a bacon slice and a few slices of mushroom.
11. Use boiling toasted potatoes to serve.

5.3 Lingonberry Jam

Cooking Time: 55 minutes

Serving Size: 7

Ingredients:

- 3½ cups Sugar
- 2.2 pounds Lingonberries

Instructions:

1. Rinse the lingonberries and pick some particulates out of them.
2. Place in the main cooking pot with clean lingonberries.
3. Add sugar and store over moderate to low heat.
4. Take it to a rolling boil. Decrease the heat and cook for at least 30 minutes or until finished. The jam would be transparent in color.
5. If the jam is set by dumping some on an ice-cold tray, and if it does not work, the jam is primed.
6. If it runs, continue to cook over medium heat for even more time and replicate the experiment until it no longer runs.
7. Then use a candy thermometer, 220°Fahrenheit, to decide whether it is set. Put some rum on the lids.
8. Load the hot lingonberry jam with the pots, seal well with the cover and turn the jars inside out to create a vacuum.
9. Store in a cool and dry position until refrigerated.

5.4 Meatballs with Celeriac and Apples

Cooking Time: 60 minutes

Serving Size: 8

Ingredients:

For the Meatballs

- 2 tablespoon breadcrumbs
- 1 teaspoon sea salt and black pepper
- 500g minced pork
- 2 eggs, lightly beaten
- 2 tablespoon plain flour
- ½ teaspoon nutmeg
- 1 small onion

For the Broth

- Sea salt and black pepper
- Small bunch of parsley
- 2 liters water
- 3 tablespoon plain flour
- 200g spelt grain
- 1 tablespoon of sea salt
- 3 apples
- 100g butter
- 3 bay leaves
- 600g celeriac
- 2 leeks
- 5 thyme sprigs

Instructions:
1. For all the other meatball components, combine the minced pork.
2. Load the water into a frying pan for the soup, insert the spice and herbs and bring it to a boil.
3. To turn the meat ball paste into balls, use a scoop to drop them into the boiling water and allow them to cook for fifteen minutes before they rise to the surface, implying that they are cooked.
4. Select them with a slotted spoon from the liquid and toss them aside. In a jug, strain 800ml of the broth.
5. Meanwhile, slice and cut the celeriac into 2 centimeters cubes.
6. Slice and drain the leeks properly. Break the apples into 1-cm-thick pieces.
7. In a big saucepan, heat the butter.
8. Add the flour and mix well, then add a little to the stored broth, stirring steadily until the sauce is creamy, without any chunks.
9. Insert the celeriac and leeks and leave to cook for 20 minutes.
10. Insert the meatballs and apple and steam until the meatballs are hot, about five minutes before the end of heating.
11. Meanwhile, in many cold-water shifts, rinse the spelt kernel.

12. Cook for 15 minutes in salted boiling water, then rinse.

13. Spray with the rosemary or chervil, eat with the spelt; prepare the meatball mixture to taste with salt and black pepper.

5.5 Kringle Recipe

Cooking Time: 110 minutes

Serving Size: 8

Ingredients:

For the Crust Layer

- ½ cup butter cold
- 2 tablespoons of ice water
- 1 cup all-purpose flour

For the Icing

- ½ teaspoon almond extract
- Sprinkles almonds
- 2 cups powdered sugar
- 1 tablespoon butter softened
- 4 tablespoons milk

For the Filling Layer

- 3 large eggs
- ½ teaspoon almond extract
- ½ cup butter (1 stick)
- 1 cup all-purpose flour
- 1 cup water

Instructions:

1. Heat the oven to 350°C. Line a baking tray or a silicone pad with baking parchment.
2. Break the butter into chunks. Combine the flour and cold bits of butter in a medium dish.
3. Cut into the pastry, using a blade or cookie cutter, until pea-sized crumbs develop.
4. Spray with ice water, then mix until a moist dough shape appears with a fork. Divide the dough into two separate parts.
5. Shape a thin strip for each part. Push on to the lined baking sheet using the back of a large beaker.
6. Combine the water and butter in a small saucepan; bring to the boil. Remove from the heat and stir in the flour instantly. Until clean, shake.
7. Add the eggs, one at the moment, whisking with each inclusion, until smooth. Integrate almond extract.
8. Split the stuffing from the crust side between the two crusts, stretching and piping up to ¾ -inch.
9. Bake for 50-70 minutes, until lightly browned and puffy.
10. Take from the oven and cool absolutely for 1 hour at the very least.
11. As the Kringle cools, the filled layer will shrink and slide.

12. Combine the icing sugar, three tablespoons of milk, oil, and almond extract in a small bowl and stir.
13. Add additional milk, one teaspoon at a time, until soft enough to sprinkle if the icing appears to be too dense.
14. Drizzle the icing on each Kringle. If needed, top with sparkles or sliced almond.

5.6 Shaved Winter Vegetables Salad

Cooking Time: 40 minutes

Serving Size: 4

Ingredients:
- Balsamic glaze
- Salt and black pepper
- 1 small golden beet
- 4 lettuce leaves
- Olive oil
- 1 purple rainbow carrot
- 4 small radishes
- 1 small red beet
- 1 watermelon radish
- 1 orange carrot
- 1 black radish

Instructions:

1. Scrub the broad radishes and the beets; however, they do not clean.
2. On the ⅛ inch position of your mandolin, cut the leafy stalk end off and cut.
3. To get the pieces just right, this may require a bit of trial and mistake.
4. Place the slices on a clean plate and cover them as you work with a damp kitchen towel.
5. Slice and dice the carrots the very same way.
6. Put a sheet of dill or leaves or two broccolis on any of 4 side dishes to arrange your salads.
7. Begin with the larger rounds in a loose stack and arrange the vegetables.
8. Place the smaller carrots on top. Sprinkle with balsamic glaze and vegetable oil.
9. Spray with salt and black pepper gently and serve straight away.

5.7 Chocolate Cake

Cooking Time: 120 minutes

Serving Size: 1 cake

Ingredients:

- ½ teaspoon grated lemon zest
- Optional toppings
- 150g sticks butter
- 2 teaspoons vanilla sugar
- 150g white chocolate

- A pinch of salt
- 2 eggs
- 150g cake flour
- 200g granulated sugar
-

Instructions:
1. Heat the oven to 180°C, first of all.
2. Next, over reduced temperature, melt the butter in a frying pan.
3. Remove from the fire and stir the squares of white chocolate until they melt.
4. The egg and granulated sugar should be beaten together until light and fluffy.
5. Use a hand-held electronic whisk or a stand blender.
6. In a separate dish, combine the flour mixture and insert softly into the egg and sugar mixture.
7. Place in the chocolate-butter and lime zest until mixed.
8. Load into the cake pan ready. Put it directly in the oven and bake.
9. Bake until the cake is only under-baked for about 15-17 minutes.
10. The core should always be very moist because it should be cooked entirely on the side.
11. As baking times can vary, keep a close eye on it. It also wants a bit more time in the oven if it wobbles.

12. Before moving to a serving tray, allow the cake to cool entirely in the pan for at least an hour.
13. If you think you have overbaked it, quickly remove it from the tin to avoid the baking process.

5.8 Finnish Salmon Soup

Cooking Time: 20 minutes

Serving Size: 4

Ingredients:

- ¼ teaspoon allspice
- Salt and pepper to taste
- 1 lb. salmon filet
- 1 cup fresh dill
- 1 cup heavy cream
- 1 lb. Russet potatoes
- 1 large carrot
- 1 large leek
- 5 cups of water
- Four tablespoons unsalted butter

Instructions:

1. Strip the salmon from the skin and cut it into large chunks. Drop and discard all tiny pin bones.
2. In a soup pot, heat the butter and sauté the leeks for ten minutes or until they are nice and fluffy.
3. Add five cups of water and the preserved fish skin in a frying pan while the leeks are frying and bring to the boil, turn the heat down, and occasionally stir for ten minutes. You can miss this phase if you are using fish stock.
4. Strain the liquid and add the potatoes, vegetables, and half of the fresh dill to the skillet with the leeks.

5. Cook for ten more minutes, just until the potatoes are only fluffy.
6. Together with the cream and allspice, add the fish chunks to the broth and boil gently over low heat until heated through just a few other minutes.
7. Insert the leftover dill and, to satisfy, salt and black pepper.

5.9 Icelandic Pancakes

Cooking Time: 15 minutes

Serving Size: 24

Ingredients:

- ¾ cup margarine
- Milk, as required
- 2 cup flour
- 2 eggs
- 1-2 teaspoon cardamom
- 1 tablespoon sugar
- ⅛ teaspoon baking soda

Instructions:

1. In a pan, combine the flour mixture. Beat the eggs in a separate mixing dish.
2. Mix softened butter and an extract of cocoa.
3. To give a thick, thin mixture, continue adding the components together.
4. Then slowly add milk if needed, and mix to produce a batter of runny texture.

5. To let everything stabilize, let the batter set for 30 minutes.
6. Butter a pan and cook until the oil is fragrant over medium-high heat; add enough batter to cover the pan in a thin layer.
7. Enable it to cook until golden brown on the rim, then turn the small pancake over on the other side to brown.
8. It is essential that you need to spin the pan as you add the batter into the pan.
9. This makes the batter scatter across the surface finely and easily.
10. Flip it on a plate to dust with sugar and cinnamon, roll up tightly until baked, or stack it on a sheet to fold in whipped cream or fruit.

5.10 Midsummer Cocktail

Cooking Time: 10 minutes

Serving Size: 4

Ingredients:

- ¼ oz. St. Germaine elderflower liqueur
- Twist of lemon
- ¾ oz. manzanillo sherry
- 1 ½ oz. aquavit

Instructions:

1. In a mixing glass filled with ice, add all the ingredients and stir for 30-45 seconds.
2. Strain into a bottle of cooled coupe and season with a twist of citrus.

5.11 Rice Pudding with Marinated Oranges and Whipped Cream

Cooking Time: 65 minutes

Serving Size: 4-6

Ingredients:

Marinated Oranges

- 1-2 tablespoon dark rum
- 2-3 oranges
- 100ml water
- 2 cloves
- 2 cardamom pods
- 90 g granulated sugar

RI's À La Malta

- ½ teaspoon vanilla bean powder
- 1-2 tablespoon powdered sugar
- 1 cinnamon stick
- 150 ml of heavy cream
- 90g short-grain white rice
- ¼ teaspoon flaky salt
- 500 ml of milk

- 200 ml of water

Instructions:
1. In a frying pan, combine the water, sugar, spices, and cardamom seeds.
2. Cook it, then boil for 6-8 minutes, stirring now and then, till the syrup is caramelized slightly.
3. Remove from heat and add the rum, and stir. Now let it cool. To extract the peel and the white rind, cut the sides of the oranges away, then shave the sides back.
4. Cut the oranges finely and put them in a dish. Pour the syrup over the orange pieces, cover the dish, and leave to marinate for at least three hours in the fridge.
5. Before serving, remove the cloves and cardamom pods. In a frying pan, put the rice, salt, and water.
6. Let it simmer and cook with the cover on for ten minutes.
7. Insert the milk and cinnamon sticks and boil gently on medium heat with the cover on until caramelized, about 30-35 minutes, swirling now and then to ensure that it does not burn.
8. Take the cinnamon stick from the flame, discard it and let it cool slightly.
9. Along with the cocoa and sugar, whisk the cream to stiff peaks and then mix the whipped cream into the rice pudding.
10. With the citrus slices and sugar, serve the ris à la malta.

5.12 Smoked Mackerel with Horseradish Cream

Cooking Time: 10 minutes

Serving Size: 1

Ingredients:

- Dill a few fronds
- Salad to serve
- Radishes 5 (sliced)
- Rye bread 2 slices
- Mackerel 1 large fillet
- 2 tablespoon white wine vinegar
- 2 tablespoon soured cream
- 1 tablespoon horseradish sauce
- 1 teaspoon caster sugar

Instructions:

1. In a pan, place the radishes.
2. Combine the sugar and vinegar, season, and spill over the radishes. For ten minutes, leave.
3. Stir and spice the mixture and the horseradish. Over the rye bread, place.
4. Place the mackerel, the soaked radish, and a little dill on top. Serve with lettuce.

5.3 Rosemary and Thyme Roasted Rsdishes

Cooking Time: 40 minutes

Serving Size: 4

Ingredients:

- Pinch of salt
- Minced chives
- 2-3 whole radishes
- Sprinkle of thyme
- Sprinkle of rosemary
- Drizzle of extra virgin olive oil

Instructions:

1. Toss the radishes with a little extra virgin olive oil, rosemary, minced thyme, and a sprinkle of salt in a cookie sheet lined with parchment.
2. Roast for around 30 minutes in the oven at 350°F. Serve with clean chives.

5.4 Jansson's Temptation

Cooking Time: 60 to 120 minutes

Serving Size: 4-6

Ingredients:

- 300ml double cream
- 2-3 tablespoon breadcrumbs
- 2 125g tins Swedish anchovies
- 300ml full-fat milk
- 60g butter
- 1.25kg potatoes
- 2 teaspoon sea salt flakes
- black pepper
- 400g 2 large onions
-

Instructions:

1. Heat the oven to 200C
2. In a large frying dish, melt four tablespoons of melted butter.
3. Insert the onions, scatter with a half teaspoon of sea salt powder, and stir over moderate heat for a few minutes.
4. Turn down the heat until they begin to lose their raw appearance, and simmer very gently for 20 minutes.
5. Keep a close eye on them, and frequently stir: they are expected to be fluffy and pale yellow.

6. You should sprinkle a little more water into the skillet if they begin to stick or add more butter.

7. Use a flexible spatula to brush them and their buttery fluids into a bowl until they are ready.

8. In the buttered bowl, put a quarter of the potatoes. Sprinkle with salt and pepper.

9. Cover the potatoes with half of the soft onions, supplemented by a tin of sprouts.

10. The second quarter of the potatoes, salt, and black pepper, as before, was accompanied by the leftover onions and the third tin of sprouts.

11. Top it with potatoes for the backline. In a container, mix the milk and butter and spill it over the potatoes. It would not cover them.

12. Push down those that poke out, only so that the fluffy milk is thinly hidden, but do not panic if they come up again.

13. If using, scatter over the breadcrumbs and scatter over the leftover tablespoon of butter, then roast for 1 hour, but examine at 45 minutes: drive the fork in and cook the vegetables if it encounters no resistance.

14. They are gold on top, for sure, but they must be soft inside.

15. The gratin can stand until required for a bit and tastes almost as well, if not better, warm instead of steamed.

Conclusion

Combined with heavy emphasis on wellbeing and ethical developmental philosophy, the Nordic Cuisine platform has a creative approach to conventional foods. Nordic cuisine, nationally and globally, will build and encourage the pleasure of cooking, flavor, and variety. Nordic dishes are typically simple, and seafood, potatoes, meat, and berries being used in many traditional meals. Fresh, raw ingredients that can be found in abundance or that come freshly from the seas are the basis of most Nordic cuisine. Nordic cuisine has so much more to it than smoked salmon and meatballs. The Nordic food culture is much more complicated than you would imagine, ranging from Norway's midnight sun to the flat, green fields of Denmark. That said, many dishes and flavorings tie all the areas together, recreating a memorable experience of Nordic cuisine. Hundreds of years of heritage and common culture have created it and a bit of Viking plunder. Nordic cuisine is straightforward, and this is called husmanskost-the farmer's fare. It is normal and genuine, made with the land's staple product. There is no reason to over-complicate things when you deal with the very finest produce of Nordic cuisine. Consider trying at least some of these beautiful Nordic dishes from the book with easy and affordable recipes.

NORDIC
COOKBOOK

70 Recipes for Scandinavian Traditional Dishes from Swedish Fika to Danish Pastry.

Maki Blanc

© **Copyright 2021 by Maki Blanc - All rights reserved.**

This document is geared towards providing exact and reliable information in regard to the topic and issue covered. The publication is sold with the idea that the publisher is not required to render accounting, officially permitted, or otherwise, qualified services. If advice is necessary, legal or professional, a practiced individual in the profession should be ordered.

From a Declaration of Principles which was accepted and approved equally by a Committee of the American Bar Association and a Committee of Publishers and Associations.

In no way is it legal to reproduce, duplicate, or transmit any part of this document in either electronic means or in printed format. Recording of this publication is strictly prohibited and any storage of this document is not allowed unless with written permission from the publisher. All rights reserved.

The information provided herein is stated to be truthful and consistent, in that any liability, in terms of inattention or otherwise, by any usage or abuse of any policies, processes, or directions contained within is the solitary and utter responsibility of the recipient reader. Under no circumstances will any legal responsibility or blame be held against the publisher for any reparation, damages, or monetary loss due to the information herein, either directly or indirectly.

Respective authors own all copyrights not held by the publisher.

The information herein is offered for informational purposes solely and is universal as so. The presentation of the information is without contract or any type of guarantee assurance.

The trademarks that are used are without any consent, and the publication of the trademark is without permission or backing by the trademark owner. All trademarks and brands within this book are for clarifying purposes only and are owned by the owners themselves, not affiliated with this document.

Introduction

As opposed to being characterized by the boundaries of a specific country, the Nordic addresses an immense region of Northern Europe, whose individuals share comparable dialects and legacy. The nations of Finland, Norway, Denmark, and Sweden altogether are called Scandinavia. Throughout the long term, these four realms battled about and exchanged land so regularly that today individuals of the locale are more comparable with one another and share numerous noteworthy associations.

The recipes and customs of every one of the Nordic nations are change yet generally speaking; they share a common root that has come to be known as Nordic cooking. Comparative plans, almost similar ingredients, and exceptionally Nordic culinary procedures all connect the different individual nations.

This cookbook contains 70 different Scandinavian recipes that you can easily follow with the help of the detailed ingredient list and easy-to-understand instructions list below each recipe. The recipe list contains breakfast, lunch, dinner, dessert and snack recipes from Sweden, Denmark, Finland and Norway.

Chapter 1: The World of Instant Pot Swedish Dishes Recipes

From Swedish fika to meatballs, Sweden has always given us some exciting Nordic recipes that are extremely easy to make at home and can complete our cravings for healthy and yummy food. Following are the recipes listed below:

1.1 Ikea Swedish Meatballs Recipe

Preparation time: 30 minutes
Cooking Time: 10 minutes
Serving: 4

Ingredients:

- Potatoes, four cups
- Soy sauce, two tablespoon
- Eggs, two
- Salt, to taste
- Black pepper, to taste
- Milk, one cup
- Onion, one cup
- Bread crumbs, one cup
- Sugar, two tablespoon

- Minced pork meat, one pound
- Beef stock, three cup
- Minced beef meat, one pound
- Minced ginger, two tablespoon
- Cayenne pepper, a dash
- Butter, two tablespoon
- All-purpose flour, five tablespoon
- Heavy cream, one cup

Instructions:
1. Take a large bowl.
2. Add the oil and onions into the bowl.
3. Add the chopped ginger into the bowl.
4. Add the minced beef and minced pork into the bowl.
5. Add the spices, eggs and bread crumbs.
6. Mix all the ingredients together.
7. Shape the beef and pork mixture into round meatballs.
8. Heat a grilling pan.
9. Add the olive oil on top.
10. Place the meatballs on top.
11. Fry the meatballs on both sides until it turns golden brown.
12. Fry all the meatballs and dish them out.
13. In a large pan, add the rest of the ingredients

14. Add the potatoes and cook them properly.
15. Add the meatballs into the mixture.
16. Cook the meatballs until dried.
17. The dish is ready to be served.

1.2 Pepparkakor (Swedish Ginger Cookies) Recipe

Preparation time: 20 minutes
Cooking Time: 20 minutes
Serving: 4

Ingredients:

- Nutmeg, half teaspoon
- Vanilla extract, one teaspoon
- Flour, three and a half cup
- White sugar, half cup
- Salted butter, one cup
- Yeast, one tablespoon
- Ginger spices, two teaspoon
- Large eggs, two
- Kosher salt, half teaspoon

Instructions:

1. Take a large bowl.
2. Add the dry ingredients in a bowl.
3. Mix all the ingredients well.
4. Add the white sugar and yeast in a bowl with two tablespoons of hot water.
5. Place the yeast mixture in a damp place.
6. Add the butter into the wet ingredients.
7. Add the yeast mixture and eggs into the cookie mixture.
8. Add the formed mixture into a piping bag.
9. Make small round cookies on a baking dish and bake the cookies.
10. The dish is ready to be served.

1.3 Swedish Apple Pie Recipe

Preparation time: 10 minutes
Cooking Time: 30 minutes
Serving: 4

Ingredients:

- Golden syrup, two tablespoon
- Butter, half cup
- Pie dough, as required
- Maple syrup, a quarter cup

- Sliced apples, one cup
- Sugar, half cup
- Whipping cream, half cup
- Butter, for greasing

Instructions:
1. In a large bowl, add the butter and beat it properly.
2. Make it frothy, and then add the sugar.
3. Beat the mixture again, and then add the golden syrup, sliced apples, and maple syrup.
4. Mix the mixture properly.
5. Lay the pie dough into a greased pie dish.
6. Add the apple mixture on top.
7. Bake the dish properly for ten to fifteen minutes.
8. Add the whipping cream on top before serving.
9. The dish is ready to be served.

1.4 Swedish Potato Pancakes Recipe

Preparation time: 10 minutes
Cooking Time: 5 minutes
Serving: 2

Ingredients:

- Fresh chopped dill, half cup
- Eggs, three
- Baking powder, one tablespoon
- Cooking oil, one tablespoon
- All-purpose flour, half cup
- Milk, half cup
- Vanilla extract, one teaspoon
- Potatoes, half cup

Instructions:
1. In a large bowl, add in the eggs.
2. Mix the eggs until a smooth mixture is formed.
3. Add in the rest of the ingredients one by one, ensuring not to form any clusters.
4. Add in the potatoes in the end.
5. Add cooking oil in a pan.
6. Add some amount of the pancake mix into the pan and cook effectively.
7. Cook the pancakes on both sides until it turns golden brown.
8. The dish is ready to be served.

1.5 Swedish Rye Bread Recipe

Preparation time: 10 minutes

Cooking Time: 20 minutes

Serving: 4

Ingredients:

- Dark rye flour, three cups
- Baking powder, four teaspoon
- Golden syrup, one cup
- Whole wheat flour, one and a half cup
- Baking soda, one teaspoon
- Buttermilk, two cups
- Sugar, half cup
- Unsalted butter for greasing

Instructions:
1. In a large bowl, add the eggs.
2. Beat the eggs until they turn creamy and frothy.
3. Add the melted butter and golden syrup into the mixture.
4. Add the sugar and beat the mixture for five more minutes.
5. In a separate bowl, add all the dried ingredients.
6. Slowly add the dried mixture into the wet mixture and fold the batter.
7. Bake the bread for ten to fifteen minutes.
8. When done, dish it out on a rack.

9. Slice the bread and add excess butter slices on top if you prefer.
10. The dish is ready to be served.

1.6 Swedish Blueberry Soup Recipe

Preparation time: 10 minutes
Cooking Time: 30 minutes
Serving: 4

Ingredients:

- Chopped white onions, one cup
- Chopped blueberries, one pound
- Chicken stock, one quart
- Unsalted butter, three tablespoon
- Dried thyme, one teaspoon
- Minced garlic, one teaspoon
- Nutmeg, half teaspoon
- Sour cream, as required

Instructions:

1. In a large pan, add the chopped onions in the butter.
2. When soft and translucent, add in the minced garlic.

3. Add thyme, nutmeg and blueberries in the stock.
4. Add in all the rest of the ingredients and cook the ingredients until the blueberries are cooked.
5. Blend the soup well.
6. Cook for an extra few minutes.
7. The dish is ready to be served.

1.7 Swedish Ligonberry Sauce Recipe

Preparation Time: 20 minutes
Cooking Time: 20 minutes
Serving: 4

Ingredients:

- Sugar, one cup
- Water, half cup
- Lingonberries, four cups

Instructions:
1. Take a large saucepan.
2. Add the berries and water into the pan.
3. When the mixture starts boiling, add the sugar and cook properly.
4. Stir the mixture well and then switch off the stove.
5. The sauce is ready to be served.

1.8 Crispy Hasselback Potatoes with Rosemary and Garlic Recipe

Preparation time: 30 minutes
Cooking Time: 10 minutes
Serving: 4

Ingredients:

- Fresh chopped dill, three tablespoon
- Dried rosemary, one tablespoon
- Salt, to taste
- Black pepper, to taste
- Mozzarella cheese, one cup
- Capers, one tablespoon
- Lemon juice, half cup
- Sour cream, as required
- Chopped garlic, half cup

Instructions:
1. Wash the potatoes.
2. Cut the potatoes in such a way so they are not separated but are attached in the end.
3. In a small bowl, add the sour cream, lemon juice, chopped garlic, rosemary, capers, salt and pepper.

4. Add the formed mixture above onto the potatoes to ensure that the mixture reaches each part of the potatoes.
5. Lay the potatoes on a baking tray.
6. Add the mozzarella cheese on top.
7. Bake the potatoes.
8. Add the fresh chopped dill on top.
9. The dish is ready to be served.

1.9 Swedish Pancakes Recipe

Preparation time: 10 minutes
Cooking Time: 20 minutes
Serving: 4

Ingredients:

- Baking soda, one teaspoon
- Unsalted melted butter, one cup
- Unbleached white flour, two cup
- Eggs, three

- Milk, half cup
- Baking powder, one teaspoon
- Sugar, a quarter cup
- Kosher salt, half teaspoon
- Maple syrup, as required

Instructions:
1. In a large bowl, add the eggs.
2. Beat the eggs until they turn creamy and frothy.
3. Add the melted butter into the mixture.
4. Add the sugar and beat the mixture for five more minutes.
5. In a separate bowl, add all the dried ingredients.
6. Slowly add the dried mixture into the wet mixture and fold the batter.
7. Mix in the milk in the end.
8. Take a large pan and heat it properly.
9. Add a little amount of batter on the pan.
10. Cook the pancake on both sides until it turns golden brown.
11. Garnish it with maple syrup on top.
12. The dish is ready to be served.

1.10 Swedish Rice Porridge Recipe

Preparation time: 6 minutes

Cooking Time: 30 minutes

Serving: 2

Ingredients:

- Rice, half cup
- Water, two cups
- Cinnamon, one or two
- Milk, one cup
- Sugar, to taste

Instructions:

1. Soak the rice in two cups of water.
2. Add three cups of water in the saucepan.
3. Add the cinnamon and mix.
4. Then boil the water for few minutes.
5. Add the soaked rice into boiling water.
6. Add the milk and sugar as required.
7. You can add the nuts and fruits in the end.
8. The dish is ready to be served.

1.11 Swedish Semlor Buns Recipe

Preparation time: 30 minutes

Cooking Time: 25 minutes

Serving: 4

Ingredients:

- All-purpose flour, four cups
- Ground cardamom, half teaspoon
- Almond paste, one cup
- Milk, one cup
- Active yeast, half teaspoon
- Eggs, three
- Sugar, half cup
- Sour cream, a quarter cup

Instructions:
1. In a large bowl, add the active yeast and sugar.
2. In a separate bowl, add in the dry ingredients.
3. Add the active yeast mixture into the dry ingredients.
4. Add the sour cream and eggs.
5. Knead the dough.
6. Make small buns and place it on a baking tray.
7. Brush the egg mixture on top.
8. Bake the buns for fifteen to twenty minutes.
9. When the buns turn a little cool, add the almond paste in between the buns by cutting a hole into the bun.
10. The dish is ready to be served.

1.12 Swedish Almond Tarts Recipe

Preparation time: 10 minutes
Cooking Time: 30 minutes
Serving: 4

Ingredients:

- Golden syrup, two tablespoon
- Butter, half cup
- Tart dough, as required
- Cream, half cup
- Almond paste, two tablespoon
- Sugar, half cup
- Sliced almond, half cup
- Butter, for greasing

Instructions:
1. In a large bowl, add the cream and beat it properly.
2. Make it frothy, and then add the sugar.
3. Beat the mixture properly, and then add in the butter.
4. Beat the mixture again, and then add the golden syrup, almond paste and sliced almonds.

5. Mix the mixture properly.
6. Lay the tart dough into greased tart dishes.
7. Add the almond mixture on top.
8. Bake the dish properly for ten to fifteen minutes.
9. The dish is ready to be served.

1.13 Swedish Visiting Cake Recipe

Preparation time: 30 minutes
Cooking Time: 10 minutes
Serving: 4

Ingredients:

- All-purpose flour, one cup
- Sugar, half cup
- Sliced almonds, half cup
- Sea salt, as required
- Baking powder, one tablespoon
- Almond powder, two tablespoon

- Vegetable oil, half cup
- Low fat milk, half cup
- Egg, two
- Vanilla extract, one teaspoon
- Cardamom powder, two tablespoon
- Almond frosting, as required

Instructions:
1. Add the dried ingredients in a large bowl.
2. In a separate bowl, add the low fat milk, vanilla extract, eggs, vegetable oil, and almond powder.
3. Mix the wet ingredients into the dried ingredients.
4. A semi thick mixture is formed.
5. Add the mixture into a baking tray.
6. Make sure the baking tray is greased properly.
7. Add in the sliced almonds on top and try to push it into the batter.
8. Bake the cake for ten to fifteen minutes.
9. When the cake is done, dish it out.
10. You can add the almond frosting on top.
11. The dish is ready to be served.

1.14 Swedish Cinnamon Rolls Recipe

Preparation time: 30 minutes
Cooking Time: 25 minutes

Serving: 4

Ingredients:

- All-purpose flour, four cups
- Ground cinnamon, half teaspoon
- Brown sugar, half cup
- Butter, half cup
- Milk, one cup
- Active yeast, half teaspoon
- Eggs, three
- White sugar, a quarter cup

Instructions:
1. In a large bowl, add the active yeast and sugar.
2. In a separate bowl, add the dry ingredients.
3. Add the active yeast mixture into the dry ingredients.
4. Add the butter and eggs.
5. Knead the dough.
6. In a small bowl, mix brown sugar and cinnamon powder.
7. Roll the dough and spread the brown sugar and cinnamon mixture on top.
8. Roll to form a log structure.
9. Cut it into thick slices and place it on a baking tray.

10. Spread the pearl sugar on top of the rolls.
11. Bake the cinnamon rolls for fifteen to twenty minutes.
12. The dish is ready to be served.

1.15 Swedish Thumbprint Cookies Recipe

Preparation time: 20 minutes

Cooking Time: 20 minutes

Serving: 4

Ingredients:

- Vanilla extract, one teaspoon
- Flour, three and a half cup
- White sugar, half cup
- Salted butter, one cup
- Yeast, one tablespoon
- Large eggs, two
- Kosher salt, half teaspoon
- Strawberry jam, as requied

Instructions:

1. Take a large bowl.
2. Add the dry ingredients in a bowl.
3. Mix all the ingredients well.

4. Add the white sugar and yeast in a bowl with two tablespoon of hot water.
5. Place the yeast mixture in a damp place. .
6. Add the butter into the wet ingredients.
7. Add the yeast mixture and eggs into the cookie mixture.
8. Add the formed mixture into a pipping bag.
9. Make small round cookies on a baking dish and bake the cookies.
10. Press the thumb in the center of each cookie before baking to make a small well.
11. Dish out the cookies when they are baked.
12. When the cookies cool down, add the strawberry jam in the center well.
13. The dish is ready to be served.

1.16 Swedish Fika Recipe

Preparation time: 10 minutes
Cooking Time: 20 minutes
Serving: 4

Ingredients:

- Baking soda, one teaspoon
- Unsalted melted butter, one cup
- Unbleached white flour, two cup
- Eggs, three

- Sour cream, one cup
- Cocoa powder, two tablespoon
- Baking powder, one teaspoon
- Chopped walnuts, half cup
- Sugar, a quarter cup
- Kosher salt, half teaspoon

Instructions:
1. In a large bowl add the eggs.
2. Beat the eggs until they turn creamy and frothy.
3. Add the sour cream and melted butter into the mixture.
4. Add the sugar and beat the mixture for five more minutes.
5. In a separate bowl, add all the dried ingredients.
6. Slowly add the dried mixture into the wet mixture and fold the batter.
7. Add the chopped walnuts in the end and fold the batter.
8. Pour the batter in a greased baking dish.
9. Bake the brownies for ten to fifteen minutes.
10. Serve the brownies with a cup of coffee.
11. The dish is ready to be served.

1.17 Traditional Swedish Glogg Recipe

Preparation Time: 20 minutes

Cooking Time: 20 minutes

Serving: 4

Ingredients:

- Bourbon, as required
- Bottled wine, one cup
- Sugar, one cup
- Ginger root, half cup
- Chopped almonds, half cup
- Salt, to taste
- Orange zest, to taste
- Raisins, half cup
- Lemon juice, a quarter cup
- Cinnamon and cardamom, two tablespoon
- Cloves, one tablespoon

Instructions:

1. Take a large saucepan.
2. Add all the ingredients into the pan.
3. Cook the ingredients for fifteen minutes.
4. The glogg is ready to be served.

1.18 Vegan Swedish Yellow Split Pea Soup Recipe

Preparation time: 10 minutes
Cooking Time: 10 minutes
Serving: 4

Ingredients:

- Chopped white onions, one cup
- Chopped blanched pea, one pound
- Vegetable stock, one quart
- Unsalted butter, three tablespoon
- Dried thyme, one teaspoon
- Minced garlic, one teaspoon
- Nutmeg, half teaspoon
- Sour cream, as required

Instructions:
1. In a large pan, add the chopped onions in the butter.
2. When soft and translucent, add in the minced garlic.
3. Add nutmeg and split peas in the stock thyme.
4. Add in all the rest of the ingredients and cook the ingredients until the split pea is ready.

5. Blend the soup well.
6. Cook the soup for an extra few minutes.
7. Add the soup in a serving bowl.
8. You can also garnish it with chopped fresh dill.
9. The dish is ready to be served.

1.19 Braised Swedish Red Cabbage Recipe

Preparation time: 30 minutes
Cooking Time: 10 minutes
Serving: 4

Ingredients:

- Fresh chopped dill, three tablespoon
- Salt, to taste
- Black pepper, to taste
- Vegetable stock, one pack
- Minced garlic, one teaspoon
- Chopped onion, one cup
- Butter, two tablespoon
- Capers, one tablespoon
- Sliced red cabbage, one pound

- Lemon juice, half cup
- Mozzarella cheese, one cup
- Sour cream, half cup

Instructions:
1. In a large pan, add the butter.
2. Add in the chopped onions.
3. When the onions are soft enough, add the minced garlic.
4. Cook the onions and then add the sliced cabbage.
5. Add salt, pepper, lemon juice and capers.
6. Cook the red cabbage properly.
7. Add the vegetable stock, sour cream and mozzarella cheese into the pan.
8. Cook the dish until the cheese melts.
9. The dish is ready to be served.

1.20 Swedish Cheese Pie Recipe

Preparation time: 10 minutes
Cooking Time: 30 minutes
Serving: 4

Ingredients:

- Golden syrup, two tablespoon

- Butter, half cup
- Pie dough, as required
- Cream cheese, half cup
- Mozzarella cheese, half cup
- Sugar, half cup
- Heavy cream, half cup
- Butter, for greasing

Instructions:

1. In a large bowl add the cream and beat it properly.
2. Make it frothy and then add the sugar.
3. Beat the mixture properly and then add in the butter.
4. Beat the mixture again and then add the golden syrup, cream cheese and mozzarella cheese.
5. Mix the mixture properly.
6. Lay the pie dough into a greased pie dish.
7. Add the cream cheese mixture on top.
8. Bake the dish properly for ten to fifteen minutes.
9. The dish is ready to be served.

1.21 Traditional Swedish Saffron Buns Recipe

Preparation time: 30 minutes

Cooking Time: 25 minutes
Serving: 4

Ingredients:

- All-purpose flour, four cups
- Raisins, as required
- Ground cardamom, half teaspoon
- Saffron thread, one teaspoon
- Milk, one cup
- Active yeast, half teaspoon
- Eggs, three
- Sugar, half cup
- Sour cream, a quarter cup

Instructions:
1. In a large bowl add the active yeast and sugar.
2. In a separate bowl add in the dry ingredients.
3. Add the active yeast mixture into the dry ingredients.
4. Add the sour cream and eggs.
5. Knead the dough and then add in the raisins.
6. Make small buns and place them on a baking tray.
7. Brush the egg mixture on top.
8. Bake the buns for fifteen to twenty minutes.

9. The dish is ready to be served.

1.22 Swedish Potato and Anchovy Casserole Recipe

Preparation Time: 20 minutes
Cooking Time: 20 minutes
Serving: 4

Ingredients:

- Olive oil, two tablespoon
- Eggs, four
- Mozzarella cheese, one cup
- Milk, half cup
- Anchovy, one cup
- Corn, one cup
- Chopped tomatoes, one cup
- Turmeric powder, one teaspoon
- Onion, one cup
- Bell peppers, one cup
- Smoked paprika, half teaspoon

- Chopped carrots, one cup
- Minced garlic, two tablespoon
- Minced ginger, two tablespoon
- Red sauce, half cup
- Potatoes, one cup

Instructions:
1. Take a pan.
2. Add in the oil and onions.
3. Cook the onions until they become soft and fragrant.
4. Add in the chopped garlic and ginger.
5. Cook the mixture and add the tomatoes into it.
6. Add the spices.
7. When the tomatoes are done, add the potatoes into it.
8. Mix the ingredients carefully and cover the pan.
9. When the potatoes are done, dish them out.
10. Mix the anchovy and potato mixture.
11. When the vegetables cool, add the eggs and milk into it.
12. Pour the casserole mixture in a baking dish.
13. Sprinkle the shredded mozzarella cheese on top.
14. Bake the casserole for twenty minutes.
15. When done, dish it out.

16. Drizzle the red sauce and sprinkle the cilantro on top.
17. The dish is ready to be served.

1.23 Swedish Spinach Soup Recipe

Preparation time: 10 minutes
Cooking Time: 10 minutes
Serving: 4

Ingredients:

- Chopped white onions, one cup
- Chopped blanched spinach leaves, one pound
- Chicken stock, one quart
- Unsalted butter, three tablespoon
- Dried thyme, one teaspoon
- Minced garlic, one teaspoon
- Nutmeg, half teaspoon
- Sour cream, as required
- Lean white fish, one pound

Instructions:

1. In a large pan, add the chopped onions in the butter.
2. When soft and translucent, add the minced garlic.
3. Add the stock, thyme, fish, nutmeg and the spinach leaves.
4. Add all the rest of the ingredients and cook the ingredients until the spinach and fish are ready.
5. Blend the soup well.
6. Cook the soup for an extra few minutes.
7. The dish is ready to be served.

1.24 Swedish Crisp Bread Recipe

Preparation time: 10 minutes

Cooking Time: 20 minutes

Serving: 4

Ingredients:

- Baking soda, one teaspoon
- Unsalted melted butter, one cup
- Unbleached rye flour, two cup
- Eggs, three
- Vanilla essence, one teaspoon
- Sugar, a quarter cup
- Kosher salt, half teaspoon

Instructions:

1. In a large bowl add the eggs.
2. Beat the eggs until they turn creamy and frothy.
3. Add the melted butter into the mixture.
4. Add the sugar and beat the mixture for five more minutes.
5. In a separate bowl, add all the dried ingredients.
6. Slowly add the dried mixture into the wet mixture and fold the batter.
7. Bake the bread by spreading a thin layer of the mixture on a baking dish.
8. Bake for ten to fifteen minutes.
9. The dish is ready to be served.

1.25 Swedish Fish Soup with Saffron Rouille Recipe

Preparation time: 10 minutes

Cooking Time: 10 minutes

Serving: 4

Ingredients:

- Chopped white onions, one cup
- Prawns, one pound
- Fennel, one tablespoon

- Potatoes, one cup
- Carrots, one cup
- Vegetable stock, one quart
- Dry white wine, half cup
- Cod, half pound
- Unsalted butter, three tablespoon
- Dried thyme, one teaspoon
- Minced garlic, one teaspoon
- Nutmeg, half teaspoon
- Sour cream, as required
- Lean white fish, one pound
- Egg yolk, one
- Bread slice, as required
- Saffron, one pinch
- Lemon juice, two tablespoon

Instructions:
1. In a large pan, add the chopped onions in the butter.
2. When soft and translucent, add in the minced garlic.
3. Add in the stock, thyme, all seafood, nutmeg and the chopped vegetables.
4. Add in all the rest of the ingredients and cook the ingredients until the vegetables and seafood are ready.

5. Blend the soup well.
6. Cook the soup for an extra few minutes.
7. Add the rest of the ingredients into a small saucepan.
8. Cook the saffron rouille and serve it along with the soup and slices of bread.
9. The dish is ready to be served.

Chapter 2: The World of Instant Pot Danish Recipes

Danish food is known for meats, rye bread, and various desserts. Customary food in Denmark depends on what could be cultivated or accumulated during the nation's short summers without much of a stretch. Following are some classic Danish recipes that are rich in healthy nutrients, and you can easily make them with the detailed instructions list in each recipe:

2.1 Danish Caramelized Browned Potatoes Recipe

Preparation time: 30 minutes

Cooking Time: 10 minutes

Serving: 4

Ingredients:

- Fresh chopped dill, three tablespoon
- Salt, to taste
- Black pepper, to taste
- Vegetable stock, one pack
- Minced garlic, one teaspoon
- Chopped onion, one cup
- Butter, two tablespoon

- Capers, one tablespoon
- Sliced potatoes, one pound
- Lemon juice, half cup
- Brown sugar, one cup
- Sour cream, half cup

Instructions:
1. In a large pan, add the butter.
2. Add in the chopped onions.
3. When the onions are soft enough, add the minced garlic.
4. Cook the onions and then add the sliced potatoes.
5. Add in the salt, pepper, lemon juice and capers.
6. Cook the sliced cabbage properly.
7. Add in the vegetable stock, sour cream and brown sugar into the pan.
8. Cook the dish until the brown sugar melts.
9. The dish is ready to be served.

2.2 Danish Meatballs Recipes

Preparation time: 30 minutes

Cooking Time: 10 minutes

Serving: 4

Ingredients:

- Soy sauce, two tablespoon
- Eggs, two
- Salt, to taste
- Black pepper, to taste
- Milk, one cup
- Onion, one cup
- Bread crumbs, one cup
- Sugar, two tablespoon
- Minced pork meat, one pound
- Beef stock, three cup
- Minced veal meat, one pound
- Minced ginger, two tablespoon
- Cayenne pepper, a dash
- Butter, two tablespoon
- All-purpose flour, five tablespoon
- Heavy cream, one cup

Instructions:
1. Take a large bowl.
2. Add the oil and onions into the bowl.

3. Add the chopped ginger into the bowl.
4. Add the minced beef, and minced pork into the bowl.
5. Add the spices, eggs and bread crumbs.
6. Mix all the ingredients together.
7. Shape the veal and pork mixture into round meatballs.
8. Heat a grilling pan.
9. Add the olive oil on top.
10. Place the meatballs on top.
11. Fry the meatballs on both sides until it turns golden brown.
12. Fry all the meatballs and dish them out.
13. In a large pan, add the rest of the ingredients.
14. Add the meatballs into the mixture.
15. Cook the meatballs until dried.
16. The dish is ready to be served.

2.3 Danish Chicken and Asparagus Tartlets Recipe

Preparation time: 10 minutes
Cooking Time: 30 minutes

Serving: 4

Ingredients:

- Mix spices, two tablespoon
- Butter, half cup
- Tart dough, as required
- Cream, half cup
- Minced garlic, two tablespoon
- Chicken, two cup
- Olive oil, two tablespoon
- Asparagus, half cup
- Butter, for greasing

Instructions:

1. Take a large pan.
2. Add the oil and chicken into the mixture.
3. Cook the chicken and add the spices and garlic into the mixture.
4. Add the asparagus into the mixture and cook it properly.
5. Cool it down once it is done cooking.
6. In a large bowl add the cream and beat it properly.
7. Make it frothy and then add the butter.
8. Beat the mixture properly, and then add the chicken and asparagus mixture in the butter.

9. Mix the mixture properly.
10. Lay the tart dough into greased tart dishes.
11. Bake the dish properly for ten to fifteen minutes.
12. Add the chopped cilantro on top.
13. The dish is ready to be served.

2.4 Danish Open Faced Sandwiches Recipe

Preparation time: 30 minutes
Cooking Time: 10 minutes
Serving: 4

Ingredients:

- Mayonnaise, two tablespoon
- Salad leaves, as required
- Cooked chicken, half pound
- Lemon juice, three tablespoon
- Avocado slices, as required
- Fresh chopped dill, one tablespoon
- Bread slices, as required
- Sugar, one tablespoon

Instructions:

1. In a bow, mix the mayonnaise, lemon juice and sugar until it forms a homogenous mixture.
2. Toast the bread slices.
3. Add the salad leaves on the bread slices.
4. Add the mayonnaise, lemon juice and sugar mixture on top of the slices.
5. Add the cooked chicken.
6. Layer the avocado slices and then the fresh chopped dill on top.
7. The dish is ready to be served.

2.5 Agurkesalat (Danish Cucumber Salad) Recipe

Preparation time: 10 minutes

Cooking Time: 10 minutes

Serving: 4

Ingredients:

- Shredded cucumber, one cup
- Shredded carrots, one cup
- Green onion, one cup
- Chopped red cabbage, a quarter cup
- Chopped green cabbage, a quarter cup
- Chopped tomatoes, half cup
- Balsamic vinegar, half cup

- Olive oil, half cup
- Chopped parsley, half cup
- Grated ginger, two tablespoon
- Lemon juice, two tablespoon

Instructions:
1. In a large bowl, add the balsamic vinegar, chopped parsley, grated ginger and lemon juice.
2. Mix the ingredients and keep it aside.
3. In the next bowl, add in the rest of the ingredients and mix well.
4. Add the dressing formed above.
5. Mix the salad and dressing.
6. The dish is ready to be served.

2.6 Danish Rye Bread Recipe

Preparation time: 10 minutes
Cooking Time: 20 minutes
Serving: 4

Ingredients:

- Dark rye flour, three cups
- Baking powder, four teaspoon

- Dried rye berries, one cup
- Whole wheat flour, one and a half cup
- Baking soda, one teaspoon
- Buttermilk, two cups
- Sugar, half cup
- Unsalted butter, for greasing
- Dark beer, half cup

Instructions:
1. In a large bowl add the eggs.
2. Beat the eggs until they turn creamy and frothy.
3. Add the melted butter and golden syrup into the mixture.
4. Add the sugar and beat the mixture for five more minutes.
5. In a separate bowl, add all the dried ingredients.
6. Slowly add the dried mixture into the wet mixture and fold the batter.
7. Bake the bread for ten to fifteen minutes.
8. When done, dish it out on a rack.
9. Slice it up and serve it with butter.
10. The dish is ready to be served.

2.7 Danish Roasted Pork Recipe

Preparation time: 20 minutes

Cooking Time: 10 minutes
Serving: 4

Ingredients:

- Fresh chopped dill, three tablespoon
- Salt, to taste
- Black pepper, to taste
- Lemon spice mix, two tablespoon
- Capers, one tablespoon
- Pork, one and a half pound
- Horseradish, one teaspoon
- Shrimps, one cup
- Heavy cream, one cup
- Mayonnaise, two tablespoon
- Dry white wine, half cup
- Olive oil, one tablespoon

Instructions:
1. In a large bowl, add all the ingredients.
2. Mix everything properly and make sure the pork is coated with the marinade properly.
3. Preheat an oven.
4. Lay the pork on a baking tray.
5. Make sure the baking dish is greased properly.

6. Roast the pork for ten to fifteen minutes.
7. In a saucepan, add the dry wine, mayonnaise, heavy cream and shrimp.
8. Cook it and then grind it.
9. Pour the sauce over the roasted pork.
10. The dish is ready to be served.

2.8 Danish Kringle Recipe

Preparation time: 20 minutes
Cooking Time: 20 minutes
Serving: 4

Ingredients:

- Vanilla extract, one teaspoon
- Flour, three and a half cup
- Heavy cream, one tablespoon
- White sugar, half cup
- Salted butter, one cup
- Large eggs, two
- White sugar, half cup (for spreading on top)
- Almond extract, half teaspoon

Instructions:

1. In a large bowl, make the pastry dough by mixing all the ingredients.
2. Make the dough and cut it into square shapes and place it on a baking dish.
3. Make sure the baking dish is properly greased and lined with parchment papers.
4. Bake the pastries.
5. For the icing, add the almond extract, cream and sugar in a small bowl.
6. Beat it well.
7. When the pastry is baked, dish it out.
8. Spread the formed icing mixture on top.
9. The dish is ready to be served.

2.9 Danish Potato Salad Recipe

Preparation time: 30 minutes
Cooking Time: 10 minutes
Serving: 4

Ingredients:

- Fresh chopped dill, three tablespoon
- Salt, to taste
- Black pepper, to taste

- Potatoes, four
- Capers, one tablespoon
- Diced anchovies, four tablespoon
- Lemon juice, half cup
- Lemon zest, one teaspoon
- Sour cream, half cup

Instructions:
1. Boil the potatoes in salted water.
2. Peel the potatoes and slice them up.
3. In a large bowl, add the salt, pepper, lemon zest, lemon juice, capers and sour cream.
4. Mix the ingredients well to form a homogenized mixture.
5. Add the boiled potatoes and diced anchovies in a bowl.
6. Pour the formed mixture on top and mix it.
7. Add the chopped dill on top.
8. The dish is ready to be served.

2.10 Danish Buttermilk Dessert Recipe

Preparation time: 30 minutes
Cooking Time: 10 minutes
Serving: 4

Ingredients:

- Buttermilk, one bowl
- Butter, one cup
- Eggs, two
- Cherries, two
- All-purpose flour, two cups
- Water, as required
- Baking soda, one tablespoon
- Salt, a pinch
- Cornstarch, half cup

Instructions:
1. Take a large bowl and clean it well.
2. Add the sugar and baking soda.
3. Add the salt and cream.
4. Mix all the ingredients well.
5. Add the beaten eggs into the mixture.
6. Add the buttermilk into it.
7. Boil the whole mixture for ten minutes.
8. Cool it down in a large bowl.
9. Refrigerate it for fifty minutes.
10. The dish is ready to be served.

2.11 Danish Breaded Pork Patties Recipe

Preparation time: 25 minutes
Cooking Time: 15 minutes
Serving: 4

Ingredients:

- Chopped garlic, two teaspoon
- Green onions, three tablespoon
- Bread crumbs, half cup
- Pork meat, two cups
- Chopped fresh dill, two tablespoon
- Vegetable oil, two tablespoon
- Salt to taste
- Cooked potatoes, two cups
- Black pepper to taste
- Eggs, two
- Chopped onions, two tablespoon

Instructions:
1. In a large bowl, add in the onions and the garlic.
2. Add in the rest of the ingredients.
3. Make round patties from the mixture.

4. Add the pork meat in the middle and cover the potatoes patties all over.
5. In a pan, heat a few spoons of vegetable oil.
6. Fry the breaded pork patties.
7. Dish the patties out when the patties turn golden brown on both sides.
8. Add cilantro on top.
9. You can serve it with any sauce that you prefer.
10. The dish is ready to be served.

2.12 Danish Red-berry Pudding with Cream Recipe

Preparation time: 30 minutes

Cooking Time: 10 minutes

Serving: 4

Ingredients:

- Redberries, one bowl
- Butter, one cup
- Eggs, two
- Cherries, two
- All-purpose flour, two cups

- Water, as required
- Baking soda, one tablespoon
- Salt, a pinch
- Whipped cream, one cup
- Cornstarch, half cup

Instructions:
1. Take a large bowl and clean it well.
2. Add the sugar and baking soda.
3. Add the salt and cream.
4. Mix all the ingredients well.
5. Add the beaten eggs into the mixture.
6. Add the red berry pieces into it.
7. Boil the whole mixture for ten minutes.
8. Cool it down in a large bowl.
9. Refrigerate it for fifty minutes.
10. Add the whipped cream on top of the pudding.
11. The dish is ready to be served.

2.13 Classic Danish Hotdogs Recipe

Preparation Time: 10 minutes
Cooking Time: 25 minutes
Serving: 2

Ingredients:

- Lemon juice, half cup
- Salt, to taste
- Black pepper, to taste
- Lemon zest, one teaspoon
- Onion, one cup
- Hotdog bread, as required
- Smoked paprika, half teaspoon
- Hotdogs, one pound
- Minced garlic, two tablespoon
- Minced ginger, two tablespoon
- Cilantro, half cup
- Olive oil, two tablespoon
- Tomato paste, one cup
- Grated ginger, two tablespoon
- Pickled cucumber, as require

Instructions:
1. Take a large bowl.
2. Add in the chopped garlic and ginger.
3. Mix the mixture and add the tomato paste into it.
4. Add the spices.
5. Add the rest of the ingredients into the bowl.
6. Mix the sauce ingredients and cook the sauce for ten minutes.

7. Fry the hotdogs.
8. Toast the bread and place the hotdog in it.
9. Add the sauce on top of the hotdog.
10. Add the pickled cucumber on top of the sauce.
11. The dish is ready to be served.

2.14 Danish Meatloafs Recipe

Preparation Time: 10 minutes
Cooking Time: 20 minutes
Serving: 2

Ingredients:

- Danish red sauce, one cup
- Salt to taste
- Black pepper to taste
- Mozzarella cheese, two cup
- Chopped garlic, two tablespoons
- Butter, two teaspoon
- Ground pork meat, two pounds
- Ground beef meat, one pound
- Cayenne pepper, two teaspoons

- Capers, two
- Cilantro, half cup
- Mix spice, two teaspoon

Instructions:
1. Take a large bowl.
2. Add the meat into the bowl.
3. Add the spices and cilantro into the meat mixture.
4. Make a loaf from the mixture.
5. Add the sauce on the loaf.
6. Place the loaf on the baking tray.
7. Sprinkle the cheese and rest of the ingredients on the loaf.
8. Bake the meatloaf for ten to twenty minutes.
9. The dish is ready to be served.

2.15 Danish Apple Pork Recipe

Preparation time: 20 minutes
Cooking Time: 10 minutes
Serving: 4

Ingredients:

- Fresh chopped dill, three tablespoon

- Salt, to taste
- Black pepper, to taste
- Lemon spice mix, two tablespoon
- Capers, one tablespoon
- Pork, one and a half pound
- Horseradish, one teaspoon
- Roasted apples, one cup
- Heavy cream, one cup
- Mayonnaise, two tablespoon
- Dry white wine, half cup
- Olive oil, one tablespoon

Instructions:
1. In a large bowl, add all the ingredients.
2. Mix everything properly and make sure the pork is coated with the marinade properly.
3. Preheat an oven.
4. Lay the pork on a baking tray.
5. Make sure the baking dish is greased properly.
6. Roast the pork for ten to fifteen minutes.
7. In a saucepan, add the dry wine, mayonnaise, heavy cream and roasted apples.
8. Cook it and then grind it.
9. Pour the apple sauce over the roasted pork.
10. The dish is ready to be served.

2.16 Danish Red Cabbage Recipe

Preparation Time: 10 minutes
Cooking Time: 25 minutes
Serving: 2

Ingredients:

- Powdered cumin, one tablespoon
- Salt, to taste
- Black pepper, to taste
- Turmeric powder, one teaspoon
- Onion, one cup
- Vegetable broth, one cup
- Smoked paprika, half teaspoon
- Sliced red cabbage, one pound
- Minced garlic, two tablespoon
- Minced ginger, two tablespoon

- Cilantro, half cup
- Butter, two tablespoon
- Crushed tomatoes, one cup
- Grated ginger, two tablespoon

Instructions:
1. Take a pan.
2. Add the oil and onions into the pan.
3. Cook the onions until they become soft and fragrant.
4. Add in the chopped garlic and ginger.
5. Cook the mixture and add the tomatoes into it.
6. Add the spices and the sliced red cabbage.
7. Mix the red cabbage so that the spices are coated all over the cabbage.
8. Cook the cabbage for fifteen minutes.
9. Dish out the red cabbage.
10. Garnish it with chopped cilantro.
11. The dish is ready to be served.

2.17 Danish Remoulade Recipe

Preparation Time: 20 minutes
Cooking Time: 20 minutes
Serving: 4

Ingredients:

- Greek yoghurt, one cup
- Dijon mustard, one teaspoon
- Chopped fresh parsley, half cup
- Mayonnaise, half cup
- Water, half cup
- Dill pickles, one cup
- Capers, one tablespoon
- Curry powder, one tablespoon
- Chopped shallots, half cup

Instructions:
1. Take a large saucepan.
2. Add the pickles and water into the pan.
3. When the mixture starts boiling, add the rest of the ingredients and cook properly.
4. Stir the mixture well and then switch off the stove.

5. The dish is ready to be served.

2.18 Danish Sillsallet (Herring Salad) Recipe

Preparation time: 10 minutes
Cooking Time: 10 minutes
Serving: 4

Ingredients:

- Chopped beets, one cup
- Herring tidbits, one cup
- Shredded carrots, one cup
- Green onion, one cup
- Chopped red cabbage, a quarter cup
- Chopped green cabbage, a quarter cup
- Chopped tomatoes, half cup
- Balsamic vinegar, half cup
- Olive oil, half cup
- Chopped parsley, half cup
- Grated ginger, two tablespoon
- Lemon juice, two tablespoon

Instructions:

1. In a large bowl, add the balsamic vinegar, chopped parsley, grated ginger and lemon juice.
2. Mix the ingredients together and keep it aside.
3. In the next bowl, add in the rest of the ingredients and mix well.
4. Add the dressing formed above.
5. Mix the salad and dressing.
6. The dish is ready to be served.

2.19 Danish Breakfast Hash Recipe

Preparation Time: 10 minutes
Cooking Time: 25 minutes
Serving: 2

Ingredients:

- Powdered ginger, half teaspoon
- Powdered garlic, half teaspoon
- Zucchini, one cup
- Apple, two
- Turmeric, half teaspoon
- Butter nut squash, one cup
- Sea salt, to taste
- Olive oil, two tablespoon
- Cinnamon, half teaspoon
- Onion, one

- Shredded carrots, one cup
- Pork, one pound
- Spinach, two cups
- Dried thyme, half teaspoon

Instructions:
1. Heat the olive oil in a pan.
2. Add the ground pork.
3. Once cooked, add in the powdered spices.
4. Remove it from the pan and set it aside.
5. Add in the butternut squash, carrots, zucchini, and apples.
6. Once they turn soft, add in the spinach as well.
7. Add the spices and cook it for five to ten minutes or until the spinach is wilted.
8. Add in the cooked pork.
9. Mix the dish well and cook for five minutes.
10. The dish is ready to be served.

2.20 Danish Pancakes Recipe

Preparation time: 10 minutes
Cooking Time: 20 minutes
Serving: 4

Ingredients:

- Baking soda, one teaspoon
- Unsalted melted butter, one cup
- Unbleached white flour, two cup
- Eggs, three
- Chopped raspberries, one cup
- Blueberries, half cup
- Milk, half cup
- Baking powder, one teaspoon
- Chopped almonds, half cup
- Sugar, a quarter cup
- Kosher salt, half teaspoon
- Sour cream, half cup
- Maple syrup, as required

Instructions:
1. In a large bowl add the eggs.
2. Beat the eggs until they turn creamy and frothy.
3. Add the sour cream and melted butter into the mixture.
4. Add the sugar and beat the mixture for five more minutes.
5. In a separate bowl, add all the dried ingredients.
6. Slowly add the dried mixture into the wet mixture and fold the batter.
7. Mix in the milk in the end.
8. Add the blueberries and chopped raspberries into the mixture.

9. Take a large pan and heat it properly.
10. Add a tablespoon of unsalted butter into the pan and when it is adequately hot, add a ladle full of the formed batter.
11. Cook the pancake on both sides until it turns golden brown.
12. Garnish it with maple syrup on top.
13. The dish is ready to be served.

2.21 Danish Scalloped Potatoes Recipes

Preparation Time: 10 minutes

Cooking Time: 25 minutes

Serving: 2

Ingredients:

- Lemon juice, one tablespoon
- Salt, to taste
- Black pepper, to taste
- Mix spice, one teaspoon
- Onion, one cup
- Smoked paprika, half teaspoon
- Potatoes, one pound
- Minced garlic, two tablespoon
- Minced ginger, two tablespoon
- Cilantro, half cup

- Olive oil, two tablespoon
- Light cream, two cups

Instructions:
1. Take a large pan.
2. Add the oil and onions into the bowl.
3. Add the chopped garlic and ginger into the bowl.
4. Add the spices.
5. Add the potatoes into it.
6. Mix all the ingredients together.
7. Cook the potatoes well.
8. Add the light cream on top of the mixture.
9. Place the pan in the oven.
10. Dish them out when cooked properly.
11. Sprinkle some cilantro on top.
12. The dish is ready to be served.

2.22 Danish Creamy Pastry Recipe

Preparation time: 2 hours
Cooking Time: 10 minutes
Serving: 4

Ingredients:

- Milk, two cups

- White sugar, half cup
- Salt, one teaspoon
- Eggs, two
- Lemon extract, one teaspoon
- Almond extract, one teaspoon
- All-purpose flour, two cups
- Butter, one cup
- Dry yeast, one cup

Instructions:
1. Take a medium bowl and add the butter in it.
2. Add the flour and mix well.
3. Then refrigerate it.
4. Take a large bowl and add the yeast into it.
5. Add the sugar, salt and milk.
6. Mix the warm milk mixture with the flour and the yeast.
7. Add the eggs, the lemon extract and the almond extract together.
8. Then knead it in the flour until the dough is formed.
9. Place butter on the dough and fold it.
10. Make pastries from the dough roll.
11. Add the heavy cream in the pastry dough.
12. Bake them for ten minutes.
13. The pastry is ready to be served.

2.23 Danish Cream Puffs Recipe

Preparation time: 10 minutes
Cooking Time: 20 minutes
Serving: 4

Ingredients:

- Eggs, three
- Sugar, six tablespoon
- Butter, a quarter cup
- Flour, one and a half cup
- Blackberries, as required
- Milk, one and a half cup

Instructions:
1. In a large bowl add the egg whites.
2. Beat the eggs until they turn creamy and frothy.
3. Add the melted butter into the mixture.
4. Add the sugar and blackberries.
5. Add in all the rest of the ingredients and fold the mixture.
6. Bake the fluffy puffs for ten to fifteen minutes.
7. Once baked, dish it out.
8. The dish is ready to be served.

2.24 Danish Dream Cake Recipe

Preparation time: 10 minutes
Cooking Time: 30 minutes
Serving: 4

Ingredients:

- Butter, one cup
- Eggs, two
- Cherries, two
- All-purpose flour, two cups
- Water, as required
- Baking soda, one tablespoon
- Salt, a pinch
- Walnuts, one cup

Instructions:
1. Take a large bowl and clean it well.
2. Add the sugar and baking soda.
3. Add the salt and cream.
4. Mix all the ingredients well.
5. Add beaten eggs into the mixture.
6. Pour into the dish and spread evenly.
7. Take a small bowl and add the sugar and butter.

8. Mix until it becomes smooth.
9. Add the mixture into the flour and mix well.
10. Bake it for about twenty five minutes.
11. The dish is ready to be served.

2.25 Danish Risalamande Recipe

Preparation time: 30 minutes
Cooking Time: 10 minutes
Serving: 4

Ingredients:

- Brown rice, one bowl
- Almond powder, one cup
- Butter, one cup
- Eggs, two
- Cherries, two
- All-purpose flour, two cups
- Water, as required
- Baking soda, one tablespoon
- Salt, a pinch
- Whipped cream, one cup
- Cornstarch, half cup

Instructions:
1. Take a large bowl and clean it well.
2. Add the sugar and baking soda.
3. Add the salt and cream.
4. Mix all the ingredients well.
5. Add the beaten eggs into the mixture.
6. Add the brown rice into it.
7. Boil the whole mixture for ten minutes.
8. Add the almond powder into the mixture.
9. Cool it down in a large bowl.
10. Refrigerate it for fifty minutes.
11. Add the whipped cream on top of the pudding.
12. The dish is ready to be served.

Chapter 3: The World of Instant Pot Norwegian Recipes

Norwegian cooking has developed lately with the flood of worldwide impact, yet the conventional food experience stays on the loose. From numerous points of view, the Vikings assumed a significant part for propensities and customs in this piece of the world, however; the mountains, waterways, sea, and crude materials accessible have molded what we know as customary Norwegian food. Following are some classic Norwegian recipes that are rich in healthy nutrients, and you can easily make them with the detailed instructions list in each recipe:

3.1 Norwegian Fish Soup Recipe

Preparation time: 15 minutes

Cooking Time: 20 minutes

Serving: 4

Ingredients:

- Fish broth, one cup
- Onion, one cup
- Heavy cream, one cup
- Fish mince, half pound
- Powdered cumin, half tablespoon

- Smoked paprika, half teaspoon
- Water, one cup
- Root vegetables, one cup
- Minced garlic, two tablespoon
- Minced ginger, two tablespoon
- Cilantro, half cup
- Olive oil, two tablespoon
- Chopped tomatoes, one cup

Instructions:
1. Take a pan.
2. Add in the oil and onions.
3. Cook the onions until they become soft and fragrant.
4. Add in the chopped garlic and ginger.
5. Cook the mixture and add the tomatoes into it.
6. Add the spices and fish mince.
7. Add in the broth.
8. Add in the root vegetables.
9. Mix the ingredients carefully and cover the pan.
10. Add cilantro on top.
11. You can serve with chopped dill on top.
12. The dish is ready to be served.

3.2 Norwegian Waffles Recipe

Preparation Time: 10 minutes
Cooking Time: 25 minutes
Serving: 2

Ingredients:

- Flour, two tablespoon
- Eggs, two
- Grated cauliflower, two cups
- Onion powder, two teaspoon
- Oregano, half teaspoon
- Salt to taste
- Pepper to taste
- Paprika, two teaspoon
- Shredded mozzarella cheese, two cups

Instructions:
1. Preheat the waffle iron.
2. Transfer the cauliflower to a bowl, and then add the cheese, eggs, flour, paprika, onion powder, oregano, salt and pepper.
3. Mix together until well-blended.
4. Spray the waffle maker with non-stick spray.
5. Add about one cup of the cauliflower mixture to the pre-heated waffle iron.
6. Cook for six minutes.

7. Remove the cauliflower waffle from the iron.
8. The dish is ready to be served.

3.3 Norwegian Meatballs Recipe

Preparation time: 30 minutes
Cooking Time: 10 minutes
Serving: 4

Ingredients:

- Eggs, two
- Salt, to taste
- Black pepper, to taste
- Milk, one cup
- Onion, one cup
- Bread crumbs, one cup
- Sugar, two tablespoon
- Minced pork meat, one pound
- Beef stock, three cup
- Minced bacon meat, one pound
- Minced ginger, two tablespoon
- Cayenne pepper, a dash
- Butter, two tablespoon
- All-purpose flour, five tablespoon

- Heavy whipping cream, one cup

Instructions:
1. Take a large bowl.
2. Add the oil and onions into the bowl.
3. Add the chopped ginger into the bowl.
4. Add the minced bacon and minced pork into the bowl.
5. Add the spices, eggs and bread crumbs.
6. Mix all the ingredients together.
7. Shape the beef and pork mixture into round meatballs.
8. Heat a grilling pan.
9. Add the olive oil on top.
10. Place the meatballs on top.
11. Fry the meatballs on both sides until it turns golden brown.
12. Fry all the meatballs and dish them out.
13. In a large pan, add the rest of the ingredients.
14. Add the meatballs into the mixture.
15. Cook the meatballs until dried.
16. The dish is ready to be served.

3.4 Norwegian Lefse Recipe

Preparation Time: 10 minutes

Cooking Time: 25 minutes

Serving: 2

Ingredients:

- Potatoes, half cup
- Full cream, one cup
- Fresh herbs, one teaspoon
- Onion, one cup
- White sugar, one cup
- Smoked paprika, half teaspoon
- Water, one cup
- Minced garlic, two tablespoon
- Minced ginger, two tablespoon
- Cilantro, half cup
- Olive oil, two tablespoon
- All-purpose flour, one cup

Instructions:
1. Take a large bowl.
2. Add the potatoes into the bowl.
3. Once the potatoes are mashed properly, add the rest of the ingredients into the bowl.
4. Knead the mixture carefully to form a dough.

5. Roll out the dough into thin tortilla sheets and cook the sheets with a little oil.
6. Add cilantro on top.
7. The dish is ready to be served.

3.5 Norwegian Surkal Recipe

Preparation Time: 10 minutes
Cooking Time: 25 minutes
Serving: 2

Ingredients:

- Apple cider vinegar, to taste
- Black pepper, to taste
- Turmeric powder, one teaspoon
- Onion, one cup
- Vegetable broth, one cup
- Smoked paprika, half teaspoon
- Sliced green cabbage, one pound
- Minced garlic, two tablespoon
- Minced ginger, two tablespoon
- Cilantro, half cup
- Butter, two tablespoon
- Crushed tomatoes, one cup
- Grated ginger, two tablespoon

Instructions:

1. Take a pan.
2. Add the oil and onions into the pan.
3. Cook the onions until they become soft and fragrant.
4. Add in the chopped garlic and ginger.
5. Cook the mixture and add the tomatoes into it.
6. Add the spices and the sliced cabbage.
7. Mix the cabbage so that the spices are coated all over the cabbage.
8. Cook the cabbage for fifteen minutes.
9. Dish out the surkal.
10. Garnish it with chopped cilantro.
11. The dish is ready to be served.

3.6 Norwegian Sveler Recipe

Preparation time: 10 minutes
Cooking Time: 20 minutes
Serving: 4

Ingredients:

- Eggs, three
- Dried raisins, one cup

- Sliced almonds, one cup
- Sliced strawberries, as required
- Sugar, six tablespoon
- Butter, a quarter cup
- Maple syrup, a quarter teaspoon
- Flour, one and a half cup
- Sliced bananas, as required
- Blackberries, as required
- Milk, one and a half cup

Instructions:
1. In a large bowl add the egg whites.
2. Beat the eggs until they turn creamy and frothy.
3. Add the melted butter into the mixture.
4. Add the sugar and crushed almonds.
5. Beat the mixture for five more minutes.
6. Add in all the rest of the ingredients and fold the mixture.
7. Bake the fluffy pancakes for ten to fifteen minutes.
8. Once baked, dish it out and slice it.
9. The dish is ready to be served.

3.7 Norwegian Potato Dumplings Recipe

Preparation time: 30 minutes

Cooking Time: 20 minutes

Serving: 4

Ingredients:

- Baking powder, a quarter teaspoon
- Cooked ham, half pound
- All-purpose flour, two cups
- Ground black pepper, as required
- Salt, as required
- Potatoes, four cups
- Melted butter, one cup

Instructions:

1. Add the baking powder, all-purpose flour, salt and ground black pepper into a bowl and mix it.
2. Peel the potatoes and mash them.
3. Add the potato mixture into the flour mixture and mix properly.
4. Add the melted butter into the mixture.
5. Form a dough from the mixture formed above.
6. Add the slices of ham into the formed dough and make small round balls.
7. In a large pan full of boiling water, add the balls and cook them.
8. The dish is ready to be served.

3.8 Norwegian Salmon with Dill Sauce Recipe

Preparation time: 10 minutes
Cooking Time: 15 minutes
Serving: 2

Ingredients:

- Bok choy, two
- Lemons, two
- Fresh basil, one cup
- Olive oil, a quarter cup
- Salmon filet, one pound
- Balsamic vinegar, four tablespoon

For Dill Sauce:

- Chopped dill, half cup
- Heavy cream, one cup
- Butter, half cup
- Salt, to taste
- Black pepper, to taste

Instructions:
1. Take a large bowl.
2. Add in all the ingredients and mix it well.
3. Cook the salmon filet by steaming.

4. You can steam salmon filet in a pan or any other dish.
5. For preparing the dill sauce, add the heavy cream into a saucepan.
6. Add the butter into the mixture.
7. Cook both the ingredients until they homogenize.
8. Add the chopped dill, salt, and pepper into the mixture.
9. Cook for five more minutes.
10. Drizzle the dill sauce over the salmon filet.
11. You can also serve the salmon with roasted or grilled vegetables dish if you want.
12. The dish is ready to be served.

3.9 Norwegian Porridge Recipe

Preparation time: 10 minutes
Cooking Time: 10 minutes
Serving: 4

Ingredients:

- Oats, two cups
- Chopped white onions, one cup
- Chopped blanched pea, one pound
- Chicken stock, one quart
- Unsalted butter, three tablespoon

- Dried thyme, one teaspoon
- Milk, two cups
- Minced garlic, one teaspoon
- Nutmeg, half teaspoon
- Celery root, two cups
- Leeks, two cups
- Lean chopped bacon, one pound

Instructions:

1. In a large pan, add the chopped onions in the butter.
2. When soft and translucent, add in the minced garlic.
3. Add in the stock, thyme, nutmeg and the split peas.
4. Add in all the rest of the ingredients and cook the ingredients until the split pea is ready.
5. Add the oats and milk into the mixture.
6. Blend the porridge well.
7. Cook the porridge for an extra few minutes.
8. Cook the chopped bacon pieces.
9. Add the porridge in a serving bowl.
10. Crumble the bacon slices and add the bacon crumble on top of the porridge.
11. You can also garnish it with chopped fresh dill.
12. The dish is ready to be served.

3.10 Norwegian Almond Cake Recipe

Preparation time: 30 minutes
Cooking Time: 25 minutes
Serving: 4

Ingredients:

- Vanilla sauce, one cup
- Butter, half cup
- Sugar, a quarter cup
- Ground cardamom, a quarter teaspoon
- Flour, one cup
- Baking soda, a pinch
- Egg, one
- Sliced almonds, one cup
- Blanched almonds, half cup

For Frosting

- Vanilla sauce, half cup
- Heavy cream, half cup
- Butter, half cup
- Brown sugar, half cup
- Cinnamon, a quarter teaspoon

Instructions:

1. In a large bowl, make the cake batter by mixing all the ingredients.
2. Make the batter and pour it into a baking dish.
3. Make sure the baking dish is properly greased and lined with parchment papers.
4. Add the almond mixture and mix up all the ingredients.
5. Bake the cake.
6. When cooked, dish it out.
7. Make the vanilla and cream frosting by first beating the butter and cream until they turn fluffy.
8. Add in the rest of the ingredients and beat for five minutes.
9. Add the vanilla and cream frosting on top of the cake.
10. Make sure to cover all the sides of the cake with frosting.
11. Cut the cake into slices
12. The dish is ready to be served.

Chapter 4: The World of Instant Pot Finnish Recipes

Finns are enthusiastic about their food, and they know exactly how to praise it. Finns are additionally furiously faithful to their culinary roots. Following are some yummy Finnish recipes that are rich in healthy nutrients, and you can easily make them with the detailed instructions list in each recipe:

4.1 Finnish Cabbage Casserole Recipe

Preparation Time: 20 minutes
Cooking Time: 20 minutes
Serving: 4

Ingredients:

- Olive oil, two tablespoon
- Eggs, four
- Mozzarella cheese, one cup
- Milk, half cup
- Red wine, one cup
- Corn, one cup
- Chopped tomatoes, one cup
- Turmeric powder, one teaspoon
- Onion, one cup
- Bell peppers, one cup
- Smoked paprika, half teaspoon
- Chopped carrots, one cup
- Minced garlic, two tablespoon
- Minced ginger, two tablespoon
- Red sauce, half cup
- Sliced cabbage

Instructions:
1. Take a pan.
2. Add in the oil and onions.
3. Cook the onions until they become soft and fragrant.
4. Add in the chopped garlic and ginger.
5. Cook the mixture and add the tomatoes into it.
6. Add the spices.
7. When the tomatoes are done, add the sliced cabbage into it.
8. Mix the ingredients carefully and cover the pan.
9. When the cabbage is done, dish them out.
10. When the cabbage mixture cools down, add the eggs and milk into it.
11. Pour the casserole mixture in a baking dish.
12. Sprinkle the shredded mozzarella cheese on top.
13. Bake the casserole for twenty minutes.
14. When done, dish it out.
15. Drizzle the red sauce and sprinkle the cilantro on top.
16. The dish is ready to be served.

4.2 Finnish Salmon Soup Recipe

Preparation time: 30 minutes
Cooking Time: 10 minutes
Serving: 4

Ingredients:

- Salmon meat, one cup
- White leeks (chopped), two cups
- Bouillon, two cups
- Black pepper, to taste
- Grated ginger, one teaspoon
- Nutmeg powder, half teaspoon
- Heavy cream, half cup
- Egg yolk, two
- Parsley, half cup

Instructions:
1. Wash and dry the spinach leaves.
2. Wash the white leeks and slice them up.
3. Boil the bouillon until it becomes tender.
4. Add the salmon meat and leeks into the bouillon.
5. Boil the dish for five minutes.
6. Add the parsley and boil the dish a few minutes more.
7. Add the salt, pepper and ginger into the dish and boil it by covering it with a lid.
8. In a small bowl, add the cream and egg yolks.
9. Mix the egg yolks properly into the cream to make a homogenized mixture.

10. Add the egg yolk and cream mixture into the soup.
11. Keep stirring the soup to avoid lump formation.
12. Add the nutmeg into the soup mixture.
13. You can place it alongside a bread slice if you want.
14. The dish is ready to be served.

4.3 Finnish Blueberry Pie Recipe

Preparation time: 10 minutes
Cooking Time: 30 minutes
Serving: 4

Ingredients:

- Golden syrup, two tablespoon
- Butter, half cup
- Pie dough, as required
- Cream cheese, half cup
- Blueberries, half cup
- Sugar, half cup
- Heavy cream, half cup
- Butter, for greasing

Instructions:
1. In a large bowl add the cream and beat it properly.
2. Make it frothy and then add the sugar.
3. Beat the mixture properly and then add in the butter.
4. Beat the mixture again and then add the golden syrup, cream cheese and blueberries.

5. Mix the mixture properly.
6. Lay the pie dough into a greased pie dish.
7. Add the blueberry mixture on top.
8. Bake the dish properly for ten to fifteen minutes.
9. The dish is ready to be served.

4.4 Finnish Meatballs Recipe

Preparation time: 30 minutes
Cooking Time: 10 minutes
Serving: 4

Ingredients:

- Lingonberry jam, two tablespoon
- Salt, to taste
- Black pepper, to taste
- Milk, one cup
- Onion, one cup
- Bread crumbs, one cup
- Sugar, two tablespoon
- Minced pork meat, one pound
- Beef stock, three cup
- Minced bacon meat, one pound
- Minced ginger, two tablespoon
- Cayenne pepper, a dash

- Butter, two tablespoon
- All-purpose flour, five tablespoon
- Heavy whipping cream, one cup

Instructions:
1. Take a large bowl.
2. Add the oil and onions into the bowl.
3. Add the chopped ginger into the bowl.
4. Add the minced bacon, and minced pork into the bowl.
5. Add the spices, lingonberry jam and bread crumbs.
6. Mix all the ingredients together.
7. Shape the beef and pork mixture into round meatballs.
8. Heat a grilling pan.
9. Add the olive oil on top.
10. Place the meatballs on top.
11. Fry the meatballs on both sides until it turns golden brown.
12. The dish is ready to be served.

4.5 Finnish Pannu Kakku Recipe

Preparation time: 10 minutes

Cooking Time: 20 minutes

Serving: 4

Ingredients:

- Baking soda, one teaspoon
- Unsalted melted butter, one cup
- Unbleached white flour, two cup
- Eggs, three
- Chopped raspberries, one cup
- Blueberries, half cup
- Milk, half cup
- Baking powder, one teaspoon
- Chopped almonds, half cup
- Sugar, a quarter cup
- Kosher salt, half teaspoon
- Sour cream, half cup
- Maple syrup, as required

Instructions:
1. In a large bowl add the eggs.
2. Beat the eggs until they turn creamy and frothy.
3. Add the sour cream and melted butter into the mixture.

4. Add the sugar and beat the mixture for five more minutes.
5. In a separate bowl, add all the dried ingredients.
6. Slowly add the dried mixture into the wet mixture and fold the batter.
7. Mix in the milk in the end.
8. Add the blueberries and chopped raspberries into the mixture.
9. Add the mixture into a baking dish.
10. Bake the pancake on both sides until it turn golden brown.
11. Garnish it with maple syrup on top.
12. The dish is ready to be served.

4.6 Finnish Pancakes Recipe

Preparation time: 10 minutes
Cooking Time: 20 minutes
Serving: 4

Ingredients:

- Baking powder, one teaspoon
- Unsalted melted butter, one cup
- Unbleached white flour, two cup
- Eggs, three
- Vanilla extract, one teaspoon
- Milk, half cup

- Sugar, a quarter cup
- Maple syrup, as required

Instructions:
1. In a large bowl add the eggs.
2. Beat the eggs until they turn creamy and frothy.
3. Add the milk and melted butter into the mixture.
4. Add the sugar and beat the mixture for five more minutes.
5. In a separate bowl, add all the dried ingredients.
6. Slowly add the dried mixture into the wet mixture and fold the batter.
7. Cook the pancake on a pan by adding a little amount of it one by one.
8. Cook the pancakes until they turn golden brown.
9. Garnish it with maple syrup on top.
10. The dish is ready to be served.

4.7 Finnish Dried Pea Soup Recipe

Preparation time: 20 minutes
Cooking Time: 25 minutes
Serving: 2

Ingredients:

- Chopped onions, one cup
- Minced garlic, one teaspoon
- Minced ginger, one teaspoon
- Peas, two cups
- Sliced bacon, ten slices
- Beer, one cup
- Water, one cup
- Smoked sausage, one cup
- Heavy cream, one cup
- Olive oil, two tablespoon

Instructions:
1. Take a large pan and heat it well.
2. Add the olive oil and onions.
3. Cook the onions until they become translucent.
4. Add in the garlic and ginger paste.
5. Add in the peas and smoked salmon.
6. Cook them properly and add a little water when the mixture dries up.
7. Add the water and beer.
8. Cook the mixture well.
9. In a separate small pan, add a little olive oil and fry the bacon slices.

10. When the slices turn brown on both sides, dish them out and let them cool down.
11. Add the heavy cream into the crockpot mixture.
12. The mixture will start to thicken.
13. When it reaches the desired consistency, dish it out.
14. Crumble the bacon slices on top.
15. You can garnish the soup with chopped cilantro or fresh chopped dill.
16. The dish is ready to be served.

4.8 Finnish Doughnuts Recipe

Preparation Time: 10 minutes

Cooking Time: 30 minutes

Serving: 6

Ingredients:

- Butter, half cup
- Eggs, eight
- Sugar, two cups
- Flour, three cups
- Milk, one cup
- Baking powder, one tablespoon
- Sour cream, two tablespoon
- Cardamom sugar, to taste
- Baking soda, one teaspoon

Instructions:

1. In a large bowl, mix all the ingredients well.
2. Form semi-thick dough from the mixture.
3. Heat a pan full of oil.
4. Make a round doughnut-like structure with the help of a doughnut cutter.
5. Fry the doughnuts.
6. Cool down the doughnuts.
7. Add the cinnamon sugar all over the doughnuts.
8. Your dish is ready to be served.

4.9 Finnish Cardamom Rolls Recipe

Preparation time: 30 minutes
Cooking Time: 25 minutes

Serving: 4

Ingredients:

- All-purpose flour, four cups
- Ground cardamom, half teaspoon
- Brown sugar, half cup
- Butter, half cup
- Milk, one cup
- Active yeast, half teaspoon
- Eggs, three
- White sugar, a quarter cup

Instructions:
1. In a large bowl add the active yeast and sugar.
2. In a separate bowl add in the dry ingredients.
3. Add the active yeast mixture into the dry ingredients.
4. Add the butter and eggs.
5. Knead the dough.
6. In small bowl, brown sugar and cardamom powder.
7. Roll the dough and spread the brown sugar and cardamom mixture on top.
8. Roll to form a log structure.
9. Cut slices and spread pearl sugar on top in a baking dish.

10. Bake the cardamom rolls for fifteen to twenty minutes.
11. Your dish is ready to be served.

4.10 Finnish Cinnamon Pastries Recipe

Preparation time: 30 minutes
Cooking Time: 25 minutes
Serving: 4

Ingredients:

For pastries:
- Butter, half cup
- Sugar, a quarter cup
- Ground cardamom, a quarter teaspoon
- Flour, one cup
- Baking soda, a pinch
- Egg, one

For the filling:
- Sugar, half cup
- Cream, half cup
- Butter, half cup
- Nutmeg, a pinch
- Cinnamon, half teaspoon

Instructions:

1. In a large bowl, make the pastry dough by mixing all the ingredients.
2. Make the dough and cut it into square shapes and place it on a baking dish.
3. Make sure the baking dish is properly greased and lined with parchment papers.
4. Cook the filling by mixing up all the ingredients for the filling ingredients.
5. Add the cinnamon mixture into the middle of the pastry and fold the pastry dough.
6. Bake the pastries.
7. When cooked, dish it out.
8. Your dish is ready to be served.

Conclusion

From Norwegian red cabbage to the Danish hotdogs' interesting taste, people from the Northern Hemisphere have vanquished the abilities expected to make the absolute most delightful food sources on the planet. The mysteries behind these kitchen brains get from a couple of old and some new Nordic style cooking strategies.

The Nordic cuisine stage has an inventive way to deal with ordinary food sources. Nordic food, broadly and worldwide, will assemble and support the delight of cooking, flavor, and assortment. Nordic dishes are commonly basic and incorporate fish, potatoes, meat, and berries utilized in numerous customary suppers.

This book covers the life of a Scandavian, making it easy for them to prepare their favorite recipes inside their kitchen without any stress. This cookbook incorporates 70 healthy plans containing Swedish recipes, Danish recipes, Norwegian recipes, and finished recipes that you can undoubtedly make at home very easily. So, start cooking today with this amazing and easy cookbook.

Printed in Great Britain
by Amazon